CONFESSIONS OF A POLE DANCING PRIEST

by
The Reverend Laura Chapman

with
Warren FitzGerald

© L. Chapman & W. FitzGerald. 2024.

Published by Armley Press, 2024

ISBN 978-1-9160165-8-3

Copy editing: John Lake

Cover: Mick Lake & Vimukthi Wanigasooriya

Formatting: Ian Dobson

Production: Mick McCann

www.armleypress.com

Dedicated to you pole dancing gods. You are amazing, beautiful, and inspire me every day. And to Spencer. It takes a strong woman to be married to a pilot, and a stronger person to be married to me.

I wish this was fiction.

Confessions of a Pole Dancing Priest

ONE

When you get a load of priests in a room together it's a quick descent, between mouthfuls of cream cake and coffee, into funeral and wedding cock-up stories. One such venue for the swapping of these ecclesiastical fuck-fails is the dining room at a ministers' retreat.

Retreat is such a soothing word, conjuring up images of incense-filled rooms in exotic settings where you take yourself voluntarily for a weekend of physical and spiritual pampering. You arrive a stressed-out mess and leave refreshed, renewed and revived. The retreats I refer to, however, are in nowhere more exotic than Stevenage, they're usually compulsory, and the only thing refreshed and revived is my will to call in sick next time. Who would choose to spend two nights and three days in a room predominantly full of white middle-aged badly dressed men, who had their suitcases packed for them by their wives, with no lifeline to the outside world since the internet has all the spare bandwidth of an overworked and underpaid single mother of four? The upside is: it's soon lunch and, after that, some free time. The downside is: I'm stuck in a schooldays canteen trying to find a like-minded soul to sit with and bitch about what's been going on this morning.

Balancing my plate of limp salad on a slippery tray without it shooting off across the parquet floor of the dining room would be challenge enough as I totter around in a cute pair of kitten heels, without the additional and very necessary task of scanning the room with all the speed of a cassocked Terminator as I turn from the buffet, it being necessary to work out quickly, while looking as if you're not working anything out at all, where to sit. Or rather who not to sit with.

Not that bloke there. I remember him from the session this morning, when we were told to walk around the garden and find something that spoke to us of the miracle of ministry. While I was wondering what the fuck that even meant, he looked as if he'd just had a great honour bestowed on him from a burning bush, and as he hopped around the garden from flower to flower, I found a rare pocket of decent Wi-Fi and got lost in a YouTube wormhole of funny cat videos.

Oh, Lord have mercy! I just made eye contact with him. And there's a place free next to him. He smiled. If I turn away now and sit somewhere else I'll look like a bitch. And worse, if there's no space anywhere else, I'll have to crawl back over there with my tail between my legs and I'll look a right saddo.

And so my legs take me exactly where my mind insisted I shouldn't go in the first place.

Thanks, legs.

Just as I'm about to sit down, my dining companion-to-be's eyes glaze over, his face twitches and I realise he's focused on something behind me. I turn and see that the something is a someone; another grey male priest – grey in aura if not in hair. I also realise in the split second that my legs bend to deposit me in the seat, that the guy behind me is the dining companion my now erstwhile dining companion-to-be was trying to make eye contact with when I got in the way.

'Oh… you're…' I said as my arse skimmed the chair and took off again like a plane aborting a landing due to a nasty wind shear – I know a bit about aviation… well, pilots… well, one particularly hot pilot. I'll tell you all about him in a bit.

'Yes, I'm… I was…' stuttered the reddening priest as his friend loitered awkwardly behind me.

'No, no, it's… I completely…' and I took off feeling like the last person to be picked for netball.

I could almost hear his sigh of relief as I skulked away. Relief that he didn't have to rack his brains for something to say to a woman, and a young one at that, and one that actually resembled a woman too. Of course, there were other female priests in this room. A few. But they tended to look and sound uncannily like the men, or like the Vicar of Dibley, as indeed did the priest I eventually found a seat next to. And, yes, it wasn't long before my new dining chums and I were bonding over those aforementioned funeral and wedding stories.

'I was just saying,' a priest who introduced himself as Graham told me, 'how I remember leading a funeral where they dropped the coffin.' He pantomimed a grimace and then chowed down on his greasy fish and chips.

'Family doing the pallbearing?' asked the Vicar of Dibley knowingly before sinking her teeth into a scone.

Graham nodded, his mouth now too full to speak.

'They should never let them do it. It's painful to watch,' I sighed.

You can't refuse, but it always makes me cringe when family members try to join the professionals with carrying the coffin – it is an intensely emotional time for them, they are naturally all fingers and thumbs and one of them inevitably faces the wrong way like an actor on parade in *Carry On Sergeant*. Then there's a whole lot of muttered, 'To me... to you,' from the men (it's always men of course), and it's at these moments that I realise the professional pallbearers present are so called not just because they bear a coffin but because they are expert in bearing with family members acting like the Chuckle Brothers shifting a piano.

Graham swallowed. 'Yes, it was most awkward,' he said, dabbing at his lips with a serviette.

'Well,' said another priest, who looked like a tortoise with a dog collar. 'I remember a wedding where the bride punched the groom for not saying I do.'

I think he might have been remembering the denouement of a Hugh Grant film he once watched and, in his dotage, real life and fiction were becoming blurred, but I didn't want to burst his bubble.

'Oh dear,' his reverend friend chuckled. 'I got the bride's name wrong during a wedding once. It was most embarrassing. Especially because I said her mother's name instead.'

'Well,' said Dibley, 'I was told by the family before one funeral that the deceased loved Queen. You know, the *rock* band?' She delighted in saying the word rock as if it was the most transgressive word she could ever utter.

The tortoise and his friend had no idea who she was talking about and Graham looked like he was only nodding to be polite.

So I said, 'Yes, Queen. I know,' to keep her picnic from being pissed on.

'Well, I'm not that familiar with their oeuvre myself,' she went on, 'so in the absence of any further guidance from the family, I just got a Greatest Hits CD and put it on as the coffin was brought in. The first song that played was called "Another One Bites the Dust".'

I winced for her and even the tortoise got it. But I wasn't done playing holy top trumps yet, so I announced to the table, 'Well, I remember a funeral where the undertaker tried to shag me in the hearse.'

If there had been a jukebox playing at this moment it would have stopped. In fact I think I heard the distant sound of Bach's Toccata and Fugue in D minor abruptly cease as the organist fell off his stool in the church next door. Teaspoons clattered onto saucers. Moustaches of cream were left unlicked. Dog collars were hidden under the double chins of gaping jaws. And yet again I found myself the object of the Church's disappointment.

TWO

Accommodation in Cambridge colleges is spartan if I were to be generous with my adjectives. Those marvellous medieval exteriors which inspire wonder in coachloads of Asian tourists year after year hide interiors which are just as medieval, but only inspire haemorrhoids. Cold, musty spaces with chairs best viewed in a Van Gogh rather than sat on. Carpetless wooden floors with cracks permitting draughts that Beyoncé could use to blow her hair back on stage, and beds which creak alarmingly, especially when you're being shagged senseless on one and the mahogany headboard is sending out a message through the limestone walls, which resounds around the cloistered court like morse code through a megaphone:

S.O.S. S-Oh-Oh-Oh-Oh-S. I won't be able to walk tomorrow. And I bloody love it.

I knew my headboard was making its announcement with all the subtlety of a pissed off carpenter, but I thought if I pretended not to hear it then no one else in the college would either – such a childlike notion to have at the least childlike of times. Besides, I wasn't going to disturb Spencer's rhythm now as I was just about to... Praise the Lord!

Spencer, though not a religious bloke, also felt the need just at that moment to call out to Jesus and then slumped down next to me, our throes giving way to the gentle tolling of a church bell; the bell from the college chapel.

'Fuck me!'

Spencer replied, 'Give me a sec.'

But this was not me demanding to go again so soon. It was me realising that that bell was the call to the evening service – the very first event of the academic year. And since I was reading theology, and this college was entirely devoted to the devotional, it was a service that wasn't to be missed.

I yanked on my knickers and threw on the nice dress I'd carefully chosen for the occasion since, after the service, it was canapés and drinks in the principal's lodge; a getting-to-know-you soirée for all the freshers in the college and their tutors. Not that I intended to stay long – after all, I had a hot, naked pilot in my bed and I couldn't wait for the second sector of the flight. Well, I was in my mid-twenties and this was my first year of university, what else are you supposed to do?

'I'll get away as soon as I can,' I said kissing him as slowly as time would allow before checking my lippy in the mirror. I'd had the foresight to do my makeup pre-shag and I offered up a prayer of thanksgiving that it was still intact as I legged it out of the room, down the stairwell, which echoed with the sound of my stilettos, and then tried not to sink them into the immaculate lawn with the DO NOT WALK ON THE GRASS sign, which in my defence I only noticed when I was halfway across.

At the chapel door, I grabbed the order of service from an impatient second year who'd been charged with dishing them out and then hurried inside.

The intention was to slip into the chapel and take a seat in the back row – always the ideal refuge for the tardy or those not wanting to be seen. However, I had never been in this chapel before and didn't realise that it – like all Cambridge college chapels, it turns out – was not your average church with pews lined up facing the front. There were just two rows of pews on either side of the nave, facing each other and the only spare seat when I arrived was in the middle of the front row on the right. The entire place could only hold about fifty people and I felt all the other forty-nine pairs of eyes boring into me as I did the walk of shame.

'No! No shame!' I told myself. 'Own it, girl!' After all, every aisle is a catwalk, right? So *tits and teeth* was my mantra as I put my shoulders back and sashayed to my seat.

In such a tiny space it could only have been a few strides to get from the door to my pew, but it seemed to go on forever, the sound of my heels on the stone floor resounding like a slow hand clap around the vaulted ceiling. Mental note, wear a nice plimsoll next time you're late for a service.

I sat down on the pew which creaked almost as much as my bed – it seemed every piece of furniture in this college was conspiring against me like the cast of *Beauty and the Beast* gone rogue. Nevertheless, I sat with all the innocent poise of Belle herself, and if I caught the eye of anyone else, my smile said, 'This glow that I'm sporting is a virginal halo, don't you know, not the ruddiness of the recently rogered.' And there was such a small number of students in the college that most of the eyes I caught were those of crusty old professors from all over Cambridge who had once studied here and delighted in returning for this important event in the academic year.

I closed my eyes and said a prayer. 'Hiya, it's me again. You told me to do this ministry malarky, so here I am. Please help me not to fuck it up and help me draw people to you. Amen. PS: please can we have some decent hymns tonight?'

The minister presiding over the service then processed down the aisle to the Communion Table, with a little less noise than I had just done, and said, 'Oh, Lord, you call us here from all corners of the world to worship you, to give you our souls and to bring you our lives. At the beginning of this new academic year, we come to give you our praise and thanksgiving in the name of Jesus Christ our Lord, amen.'

'Amen,' we all chorused.

And the minister added, 'We now stand together and sing hymn number thirty-six, "God is Here as We his People".'

Acceptable opening tune. Not a banger, but I'll take it. Thank you, Lord.

As the organ blasted out the introduction to the hymn, I stood along with everyone else and took a deep breath readying myself to sing, but was silenced immediately by the sensation of what felt like a litre of Spencer's semen seeping out of me and into my knickers. I clenched, but it was too late.

'Shit,' I hissed and the eyebrow of the second year next to me raised piously.

Trying to concentrate on and participate in a church service with jizzy knickers is not the nicest feeling, especially with the constant standing up and sitting down which made for a cold soggy reminder after every hymn of my faux pas and made me paranoid that whoever was sitting behind me might soon see evidence of it seeping through my very lovely Ted Baker dress. As soon as the service was over I got up, checking the pew for snail trails, and, satisfied I hadn't yet soaked my dress, I made for my room.

'This way!' said the croaky voice of a sixty-a-day smoker.

I turned to see the prune-like face of whom I soon knew to be my personal tutor, Dr Madeline White, hot on my heels.

'Drinks in the principal's lodge now,' she said. It sounded more like an order than an invitation.

'Blimey! If you're here, who's ruling Narnia right now?' I thought, as her wand-like fingers clutched my elbow and led me towards the principal's residence. 'Oh, yes,' I said. 'Oh shit,' I thought. 'Of course,' I said. 'I thought it was this way,' and I pointed longingly towards my room. 'Still not sure of my way around yet,' I tittered awkwardly.

She tittered not.

I would have to meet with Dr White every six weeks or so. Your personal tutor was there to keep a check on you; make sure you were keeping up with the work of your degree, but also to make sure you were on top of all the practical, religious elements of the job of being a priest, which was after all what you were there to become. She'd make sure you were attending morning chapel enough times, participating in the life of the college and that you weren't found shagging on the college lawn or staggering back home at two in the morning, or worse perhaps, staggering into lectures. Madeline would be the one who would report to a special panel every term on your progress. Because you didn't get to see what she'd written, it was worse than the end of year report card you'd take home to your parents in secondary school after trying unsuccessfully to turn the C into an A with a leaky fountain pen. And although the advent

14

of GDPR makes me want to stick pins in my eyes every time I arrive at a new website which asks for my permission to stalk me, at least it means we're entitled to see the reports written about us these days.

The panel was known as the McPoc. I know it sounds like a particularly gross burger, but in fact it was an acronym which stood for Ministerial Candidates' and Probationers' Oversight Committee. This panel would decide, based on your personal tutor's report, if you were worthy of continuing the course or not, so it was in my interest to keep Dr White on side. Personal tutors were also there to look after your well-being, but as you will see, that seemed to be bottom of the list of Madeline's priorities.

So there I was standing by a beige buffet, glass of red wine in hand so oaky I might as well have been sucking on a tree, trying to work out if any of the doors in the wood-panelled walls led to a toilet where I could dry out these sodden knickers of mine.

Principal David Tanner's lodge was an incredibly sumptuous and imposing place compared to the student accommodation. Three of the four walls of his living room were lined from floor to ceiling with books, dark leather-bound tomes, each of which I imagined it would take a lifetime to read so I was pretty sure they were just there for show; Chesterfield chairs and sofas, none of your piles-inducing nonsense in here; Persian rugs and warmth. It was a miniature Downton Abbey.

Not yet sure which of the doors I needed to slip through, I absentmindedly picked up the nearest foodstuff, a sausage roll that looked as if it would be bullied in a boys' changing room, and stuffed it into my mouth. I was so hungry after my bedroom workout that for a regrettable moment my vegetarianism took a back seat. I tried to appear refined, but it's hard to balance a glass of wine, a paper plate and napkin in three-inch stilettos on wood, especially because my legs were still a bit wobbly from my earlier tryst. And, as if he had been waiting for me to fill my mouth, the principal himself appeared at that very moment and started small-talking at me; something, I would come to learn, he did very badly, which is unfortunate for a minister whose job it is to be good with people. His timing, I would also learn, was always this atrocious.

'Which part of the world do you hail from, then?'

I wanted to answer promptly so as not to seem ignorant, but that would have involved spraying processed puff pastry in his face, so I decided to swallow as quickly as I could and for the next five minutes felt a hideous bolus of sausage meat working its way far too slowly down my throat

'Me?' I squeaked. 'Oh, I come from the Midlands,' I said.

If anyone would know where the toilet was in the principal's lodge, I thought, it would be the principal, but it wouldn't be good form to excuse myself so early in the conversation, although now I had two reasons to find it: drying my knickers and throwing up this lump of stuff sourced from a meat factory floor.

'Ah. Splendid. Yes, I thought I detected an *accent*,' he said knowingly, condescendingly.

I was dying to point out to him that he too had an accent, that we all have an accent, but his plum in the mouth and rod up the arse one was considered, by those who spoke with it at least, to be the only true version of the language and therefore indicative of a higher social standing. Bell-ends. But I thought that wouldn't be good form either, especially on my first day.

'How's the wine?' he said, nodding at my glass.

'Oh lovely, thanks,' I said as if I was talking to every waiter who'd ever asked in every restaurant I'd ever been in no matter how shit the food was.

'David, this is lovely paté. Wherever did you get it?' the owner of the arched eyebrow who'd sat next to me in chapel lied in her efforts to kiss the principal's arse, thereby inadvertently giving me a moment to escape as David went on to describe in detail exactly which farm in Provence was responsible for force-feeding a goose until its liver had exploded out of its body to produce his favourite amuse-bouche.

I edged my way through the small groups of students all painfully trying to show off their education and holiness while impossibly appearing likeable at the same time until I found my way into the hallway. I spotted a black and white tiled floor peeking out from under a half-open door and thought it must be either the kitchen or the bathroom. To my crotch's delight it was indeed the bathroom.

'Thank you, Jesus,' I mouthed to the heavens.

Once safely locked inside, I went about trying to blot my knickers dry with fistfuls of toilet paper, but all I succeeded in doing was to inset my gusset with clumps of irritating tissue, so that, after a while, before someone else came along wanting to use the facilities, I decided to take off the offending underwear altogether and dump it in the bin, hoping to God no one would notice a pair of black lace Victoria's Secret panties among the used cotton wool pads and empty toilet rolls.

'Farewell, old friend! You've served me well. We return the mortal remains of this beautiful underwear to the earth. May it rest in peace.'

At last, going commando, I slinked out of the bathroom preparing to concentrate on getting to know my fellow students and tutors. However, as I did, a vision arrested me in the corridor. It was a vision almost as stunning to me as the sight of God's flaming and naked body was to Ezekiel. Yes, body. God has one, complete with genitals, but we'll get to that later. Right now the corporeal magnificence I beheld also appeared, at least at first, to be of the heavens. Two globes, clad in paisley, seemed to be floating towards me. They were, it turned out, the biggest pair of tits I had ever seen, held up splendidly by a bra which must have had its own planning permission, making them protrude so far ahead of their owner that they were in a different time zone. When she eventually caught up, I could see the woman they were attached to was grey haired, with large cheeks rouged not by make-up but rosacea. Her small eyes twinkled as if delighted, but her tight mouth seemed to disagree with them. Her head was held high and her shoulders back, which was just as well otherwise she might have tripped on that awe-inspiring bosom of hers, clad, as the rest of her body was, in a beautiful flowing kaftan or three. Part of me wanted to give her a round of applause and part of me wanted to run and hide.

She looked down her nose at me and said, 'Are you all right, dearie?'

I nodded frantically while I found my voice. 'Yes, yes. I am now I've... spent a penny.' I cringed at my coy language, but I felt so intimidated while simultaneously wanting to bury myself in her boobs – I bet you could sleep so well in there.

'Well, let's get this tediousness over with, shall we?' she said with a wink and wafted into the living room.

I followed her inside and watched, entranced, as she stalked about the place as if she owned it. I realised it wasn't just me she looked down her nose at; she looked down her nose at nearly everyone, but that was only because she never stooped, never let that fine posture sag for a moment. Everyone seemed to cow before her, including David who scurried about the room, bringing her wine and food, simpering as he did so.

'Who *is* that?' I said to another fresher.

'David's wife. Charlotte,' they said. The fresher in question had not given their pronouns as they/them, I just have no idea to this day what gender they were as I couldn't take my eyes off Charlotte.

It was only a few cheese puffs and a twiglet later that Charlotte rolled her eyes and left.

I lasted about five minutes longer than her.

Well, it was either make more small talk or get back to the hot, naked pilot for one more ride before he had to go off to the airport for work. I mean, what's a girl to do?

THREE

The hot, naked pilot in question was my boyfriend. Sort of. We had met when I'd been living somewhere in the British outback – or the Fens as it's more commonly known. I was what my church calls a lay worker – basically a priest without the house or the outfit and on half the pay. I was also a local preacher at the time, which is the job you must do first if ultimately you want to be a full-on bona fide priest. It's work experience, if you will, to demonstrate that you can preach and take a Sunday service, and something which you have to do before you can go off to college and 'candidate' or train as a minister. Being a lay worker is optional, great practice but not essential; becoming a local preacher is a dealbreaker and a must. In my denomination, priests often have more than one church to look after and services typically take place in all churches at the same time on the same day (that's a Sunday, if you were thinking about popping in) so a priest will often need someone to take another service in their place – this is where the local preacher comes in handy.

During my time as a lay worker, when I decided I definitely wanted to take the leap and become a priest, I had to create a portfolio of essays and reflections, as well as evidence of work experience both as a lay person and working alongside a priest and deacon. Eventually, after a year or so, you sit before three panels, which become more and more intense the further you get. The first was a mere local panel – no worries. Then a district panel; a whole day of giving presentations and answering questions – slightly more nerve-wracking. Then, should you pass that, there was a twenty-four-hour grilling, and I was bricking it because this was an intense interrogation, a brutal picking of your brain, which even included a psychiatric test – 'Tell me about your relationship with your father', you know, the whole Freudian nine yards.

About halfway through this inquisition, this make-or-break moment on the path to my vocation, my mum decided now would be the perfect time to message me with the news that my brother had decided to emigrate with his very new partner and was leaving the country in two days' time. Now, this was of course urgent news that I would absolutely insist on knowing about, but could it have waited a few hours more until I had finished the most important interview of my life? Probably.

It was typical of my mum, typical of my dysfunctional parents, hence when I was on the psychiatrist's couch and he asked me about my family, I was a little too honest.

'My father's an arsehole. And my mum… How long have we got?'

Needless to say, perhaps, I didn't pass the psych test.

After an emotional chat with the chaplain, we decided I should go home to say the big goodbye to my brother, because who knows when I might see him again? Actually, I saw him just six weeks later when he came home saying life overseas wasn't for him. So I had jeopardised my whole life plan, my calling, no less, for what turned out to be a holiday in the sun and my honesty about my maladjusted family.

Luckily, I was allowed to see another shrink, who gave me a chance to not be as honest about my family and convince her that, unlike every other human being on the face of God's green earth, I had no issues. And so she declared that I was fit to train as a priest. Hallelujah, praise the Lord!

I received the good news in June and term started in September in Cambridge, so I could kick back and celebrate with my friends for the rest of the summer. And, to get the ball rolling, just at that moment an invitation came through the door from my neighbour, who was celebrating his birthday with a great big house party for friends and family, which all the neighbours were invited to as well.

I didn't know anything about this guy really – apart from the fact that he was recently divorced, which I think was partly the reason why the party was going to be such a blowout – so I didn't want to turn up on my own. But I knew someone who would be up for coming along – my good friend Florence or, as she was affectionately known, Flo-job.

'You've never had a blowjob until you've had a Flo-job,' she would argue.

I, I'm afraid, can't attest to that.

She met me at my house on the night of the party at about 9:30 p.m. as I'd had to lead a Bible study group earlier that evening, so by the time we got to the party it was banging and we were playing catch-up. That's why, as the DJ mixed Rihanna into Soulja Boy, Flo-job and I stood in the kitchen downing as much of the wine we had brought as we could in order to become as uninhibited as the rest of the people cutting shapes on the living room shag pile and snogging on the three-piece suite, until there was a tap on my shoulder and a masculine growl saying:

'Who are you?'

I turned to see the birthday boy, Spencer, a hot, and as yet, fully clothed, pilot.

'It's me. From across the road. You invited me. And this is Flo-j— I mean Florence.'

Spencer looked me up and down, taking in my bootleg jeans, my sparkly gold belt, my pink sleeveless top (ribbed for extra pleasure) with a plunge so low my navel could feel a draught. It took him a long while to equate this vision before him with the religious nut job over the road, whom he'd assumed would never come.

'Oh!' he slurred when the penny dropped. 'You're the vicar person.'

'That's me.' I cringed. 'The vicar person.'

Spencer proceeded to ask me all sorts of questions about my job, when all I wanted to do was get drunk and get on the dance floor. And for a good twenty minutes he was yakking away at me until, mercifully, a friend of his dragged him to the karaoke to have a go at 'Living on a Prayer'. Once more left by the fridge with our wine, Florence and I finally caught up with the rest of the guests, and by about 1 a.m. – you know, that time of night, after a few hours of necking copious amounts of booze, when all the best decisions are made and when all the greatest ideas are born – I said to Flo-job:

'I've got a great idea. Let's go upstairs and find his porn!' My eyes gleamed as if I'd just come up with a suggestion for proving string theory.

'That sounds like a very bad idea,' said Flo-job. 'What if we get caught? We're bound to get caught.'

'Why would we get caught? Everyone's busy down here having a good time.'

'They might notice us go upstairs.'

'We say we're just going to the toilet,' I slurred.

'And if someone else comes upstairs to use the toilet?'

'We'll be quiet. They won't know we're there. Come on!' I said, dragging her with me as I stumbled up the stairs and found the master bedroom.

'Yellow sheets,' I said, squinting in the gloom, since we'd decided not to draw attention to ourselves by switching the light on. 'Nice.'

'Any jizz stains on them?' Florence said.

We pulled back the duvet and inspected it critically. How ironic that I was quite prepared to be disgusted if I found any and yet, a few months later, a river of the very same man-milk would be flowing out of me in a Cambridge college chapel service.

'Well, he's clean, I'll give him that,' Florence said, seemingly disappointed.

'Now,' I scanned the room, 'if I were a middle-aged pilot where would I hide my porn?'

'I'll check the drawers,' Flo said and began rifling through Spencer's pants and socks.

And then, with a flash of inspiration, I shouted, 'Under the bed,' as I recalled the place my brother used to hide his.

So as Florence worked her way through the underwear, I got on all fours and stuck my head under the bed, padding my hands around like Bartimaeus before Jesus gave him back his sight. However, whereas Jesus told the newly seeing beggar that his faith had made him well, I was flailing around blindly because the booze had made me unwell – in the head at least.

But just then things got a lot clearer as the light came on and I heard Spencer's voice calmly saying, 'What are you doing?'

I froze. And even though my arse was sticking out from under the bed, I thought – a bit like when I tried to fool myself that no one else could hear us shagging at college – that if I stayed very still, he'd never know I was there.

Flo-job too had frozen, but since she was standing next to the door there was little chance she wouldn't be noticed, unless Spencer had a floor lamp the shape of a big-breasted young woman. My booze-addled brain decided that this was indeed a possibility and that we were both quite safe as long as we remained stock-still, until I heard Florence say, 'Um… well, you see…'

My friend was clearly not as adept at impersonating furniture as I thought I was, so I had to come to her rescue, as good friends do. I shimmied out from under the bed and shouted over the thud of the rock song from below, 'We're looking for your porn, of course.' Despite what I'd learned on the psychiatrist's couch at the inquisition, I thought honesty was the best policy here.

'I don't have any,' Spencer said patiently, instead of just kicking us out, as he probably should have.

'Bullshit,' I replied.

'No, I really don't,' he said looking amused and a bit bemused that he'd just caught the *vicar person* under his bed looking for X-rated publications.

'Of course you do,' I insisted. 'Every bloke does.'

'Why would I have porn mags under my bed? This is 2008,' he said coolly. 'We have the internet these days.' He gestured to his laptop.

'Oh yeah,' said Flo.

'Oh yeah,' I said, feeling suddenly sober and more old school than the AC/DC tune pumping up from downstairs. I felt as if I'd totally humiliated myself, so it was only minutes later when Florence and I slipped out of the party and staggered over to my house, where we made bacon sandwiches, the perfect drunk sponge, and while I sat on the toilet eating mine Flo-job lay in the empty bath stuffing her face as we conducted a debriefing on the evening's events.

'I'll never be able to look him in the face again,' I sighed.

'That'll be difficult, what with him living right opposite,' Flo said, her words muffled by a wad of greasy bread.

'Yeah. Literally opposite, like I can see what he's watching on telly when I do the washing up.'

'There's no escape, then.'

'I know,' I said. 'I'll have to move.'

'You are moving soon. To Cambridge.'

'Oh yeah. But that's still a couple of months away.'

We both pondered on this, chewing sagely on our sarnies for a moment. Then Florence piped up, 'The pros and cons of anal sex. Discuss.'

So we did. And I forgot for a while about my shameful behaviour…

…Until there was a knock on the door one day. I opened it expecting it to be an Amazon courier asking me to take in yet another package for Ben at number 36 – the drawback of not working a regular nine to five. But it was Spencer.

'Hey,' I said, feeling my face get hot.

'Hey.'

'Hey,' I said again. I'm usually more loquacious than this, of course, otherwise my sermons would be a little on the brief side.

'Just wondering if you fancied popping round for a drink and a chat,' he said.

'What… now?'

He nodded. 'If you're free, of course.' A small cloud of self-consciousness scudded across his face and I suddenly remembered his recent divorce.

'*Oh*,' I thought, 'he needs some pastoral counselling. He's obviously been through the mill recently. Make yourself available to him!' I ordered myself. 'This is your chance for redemption.'

And so I went across to the scene of my previous misdemeanour and he poured me a glass of wine.

'How *are* you?' I said, softly, showing him I was ready to listen.

'I'm great,' he chirped.

'Oh.' That wasn't quite what I was expecting, even though I was glad to hear he was doing well.

As he continued to chat and we continued to drink and he continued to shuffle closer to me on the sofa, I quickly realised pastoral counselling was the last thing he had asked me to come round for.

'Well, he is hot,' I said to myself. 'And, as it turns out he hasn't called me here to minister, so technically I'm off duty.' Because, of course, as a priest one never shags the sheep. No! Fucking the flock is out of the question. 'He isn't even a Christian, let alone part of my congregation,' I told myself, 'so that makes him fair game, right?'

Right.

Before I knew it, I saw those yellow sheets up close again, but this time I was on top of the bed rather than under it.

In the afterglow, pillow talk ensued and though we were both keen to see more of each other Spencer made it clear that, after the complicated and horrible experience of his former relationship, he didn't want anything heavy. This suited me down to the ground because, as I told him, I was moving away to college in a couple of months and my previous relationship was also a bit of a train wreck, so why don't we just have a few months of fun, dates and more of that great sex we'd just had, please? A summer lovin', casual, no strings attached relationship. The day I moved to Cambridge would be the day we ended whatever this was. Perfect. Hot sex, someone to go out to the cinema or a meal with, and no drama or emotional baggage.

So that's what we did.

Taking all that pressure and all those expectations off our shoulders meant that the ensuing weeks were beautiful, glorious, amazeballs. But when it came to say goodbye, neither of us wanted to lose that beauty, glory and... those amazeballs.

We decided that, since he was flying out of Stansted regularly at the time, Cambridge would be on his way home, so why not pop in to my college en route to break up the journey, and have a bit more fun?

And so there we were, having a bit more fun on my creaky bed while the rest of my fellow undergrads were eating swollen goose entrails, dyeing their teeth black with the cheapest Bordeaux and debating with the mothballed David Tanner and the dried-up White Witch whether it was time to have a new hymn book for the church and if so what should be in it.

FOUR

It was Freshers' Week and, along with newbie students up and down the country, I found myself attending all manner of inductions, orientations and ice-breaking social events, the first of which was a Saints and Sinners party.

Now, the Saints and Sinners parties I had attended in the world outside theological college were usually great excuses to get dressed up and act like a slut. They consisted of a lot of horned and horny devils, half-naked catwomen in black tights and heels, a naughty nun or two and whole lot of sinning. However, I had a feeling the college one would tend to lean more to the saint side, so, inspired by my pilot boyfriend, who I'd be bringing along to the party, I decided to go as Joseph of Cupertino, the patron saint of aviators. But a cassock and halo was just too depressing to consider as my costume, so with Spencer's pilot hat and one of his shirts resplendent with epaulettes as my concession to toning it down, I donned a pair of fishnet tights and three and a half inch heels and burst into the party.

Wrong room.

Fat load of use that orientation session was. I was in fact next door to the party in a room the college had hired out to the local Jewish society.

'Sorry,' I said demurely to the kippah'd gents inside, and scurried out.

When I entered the correct room I considered going back to the Jewish society as their conservative meeting looked more fun. There were about a dozen people at the party and nearly all of them were in cassocks. Luckily I'd had plenty to drink before I came out so I was ready to deal with anything. I marched straight up to the nearest person and said, 'Who are you meant to be?'

'Judas Iscariot,' he sighed. I think I was the twelfth person who'd asked him that.

'Oh yes I see,' I lied. 'I love the comedy facial hair. Very Biblical.'

27

'That's my normal beard,' he mumbled.

I thought it was time to mingle a bit more.

'Hey, St. Joseph of Cupertino,' said the lovely gay guy I'd met the day before. 'G and T?' He handed me a glass. He had nice chiselled features and extremely tight blond curls, which made him look the spit of a bust of Emperor Hadrian, who as it happened was famously partial to a bit of bum too.

'How on earth did you know who I came as?' I smiled.

'Some people geek out on Star Trek. I geek out on saints.'

'Did *you* bring the gin?' I asked, gratefully guzzling mine. He nodded.

'Thank the Lord for you. I couldn't bear another glass of the shit wine the college serves up.'

'Well, most of them are teetotal. They wouldn't know a good wine if Saint Vincent himself handed it to them.'

'Patron saint of wine?'

'Well done!' he grinned. 'Thought you were bringing the boyfriend to this?'

'He's coming. His flight was delayed, but he'll be here any minute,' I said hoping that was true.

'And you've come as...' I said inspecting the red arrows stuck all over Emperor Hadrian's cassock.

'St Valentine, of course,' he cried, giving me a beautiful twirl.

'Of course, of course,' I laughed, wincing at the thought of poor Valentine, who was executed for refusing to deny Christ and for ministering to persecuted Christians.

Hadrian – for that's how he was henceforth known – and I chatted easily and began to bond quickly. We shared some more gin as we surveyed the room and were just beginning to bitch about the poor effort of the woman who'd come in her husband Andrew's clothes, claiming she was St Andrew, when Spencer entered the room. Dressed as Hitler.

I flew, as fast as the patron saint of aviators might, across the room, bundled him back out and down the corridor.

'What?' he protested.

'You can't come dressed like a Nazi!' I hissed.

'Why not? It's a Saints and Sinners party. Who's more sinful than Hitler?'

'I know, I know, but, one: you're not Prince Harry, and two: the Jewish society is right there,' I said, flinging a thumb at the room we'd just hurried past.

'Oh, I know,' Spencer said wearily.

'You know what?' I said, distracted for obvious reasons. 'I got the wrong room and went in there first.'

'Oh, so did I... you *what?*'

'Yeah, but the worst bit was, I was so embarrassed, as I left I waved goodbye.'

'Why is that the worst bit?'

'It's amazing how a wave can look like a fascist salute when you're dressed like this.'

Trying not to imagine the moment Spencer described, I said, 'We have to find you something else, quick!'

I smuggled the confusingly hot Nazi back to my room, praying I wouldn't bump into the White Witch or the principal or in fact anyone. Once safely inside, we stood there thinking of an alternative that we could make from whatever we had lying around until there was a knock on the door.

'Shit! Who's that?' I whispered. I ordered Hitler into the cloakroom and opened the door a crack.

It was Hadrian.

'Thank God. I thought it was a tutor.'

'Thought you might need some help with an alternative costume,' he smiled.

'Ah, bless you,' I said with great relief until Hadrian shwed me the leather BDSM mask and thong he had brought.

'No way!' Spencer said, poking his head out of the cloakroom.

'Where on earth did you get that?' I laughed, feeling much more relaxed all of a sudden.

Hadrian reddened ever so slightly. 'Oh, just had it in case the St Valentine costume didn't work out.'

'Yeah, right!' I giggled.

'I know!' said Spencer, suddenly resourceful when faced with the prospect of going as a gimp.

He found a stripy Ralph Lauren top in his suitcase, cut eye holes out of the sleep mask he had taken from the plane and voila! A burglar. Now I could return to the party with a character on my arm who was the right side of sinful. After all, the two men that were crucified with Jesus were robbers.

Back at the party I was aware how awkward most of my fellow students were around Spencer – and it wasn't because of his costume. I could see that knowing he wasn't a Christian unsettled them somehow. They didn't know how to approach him because, to them, he didn't fit, much like their saggy corduroys and knitwear. They weren't sure what to talk to him about and it made me want to shake them all and say, 'For fuck's sake, people, he's a person, like you and me. And if you can't talk to someone who isn't a Christian then you're going to crash and burn pretty quickly when you're ministering in the real world, because that's what we have to do – talk to people.' Talking to people was, for me, one of the biggest attractions of becoming a priest – that and the free house and the escape from the 9-5, of course. I'm super nosy so what better job to have than to ask questions and get to know people.

Spencer handled it all in his usual, pilot-cool-under-pressure way, but as term went on he revealed to me that he anticipated I might ditch him one day for a nice Christian boy. I soon put him straight on that. The only boy in college I was remotely attracted to was Hadrian, and that certainly wasn't a sexual attraction – and even if it were, it would never be reciprocated. Nevertheless, Spencer felt the need to acquaint himself a little better with the Bible, so that he could talk to me about my studies and work, if nothing else. He'd been to church twice in his life: once to get married to his former wife and once when he was baptised, and, since he was two at the time, that didn't really count. Now, surrounded every time he visited me by churchly things, he started to ask a lot of questions. But the questions he asked were more philosophical than theological, so I directed him not to the Bible, but to Plato's *Republic*. In that text published nearly four hundred years before Christ, he read Plato's theory that if a person ever existed who was the paragon of generosity and selflessness, a purveyor of wisdom and a teacher of true spiritual enlightenment, then that person would be at such odds with the flawed society we live in that their perfection would be mistrusted and misunderstood, and so they would be persecuted and eventually eliminated by the authorities and those that feared change. It was a bit of an epiphany for Spencer. Suddenly the fantastical story of Jesus and his crucifixion started to make real, logical sense to him. With *Republic* in one hand and the Gospel in the other, Spencer found what he was looking for and that is why today Spencer would describe himself as a Christian. Although the church would probably not, because he, like me, questions the establishment and its fusty outdated ways. Something that I was soon to find out would be more than frowned on by the pious pricks in charge of my college education.

FIVE

Like most religions, Christianity has often missed the point of its own existence over the millennia – the point surely being unity – and divided itself into sects and subsects, into tribes, if you will, that are little better than gangs, at best critical of each other and at worst deadly. The rather tamely monikered *Troubles* of Northern Ireland are a prime example on the doorstep of our ironically named United Kingdom. Go back just a little further and we were burning each other at the stake. So I thought it was a great idea that once a month all of the theological colleges in Cambridge, no matter what denomination, would get together for one massive service. This Christian Federation, I thought, was a fine nod towards ecumenism as Anglicans, Methodists, Catholics, United Reformists and even Eastern Orthodox Christians came together, with a different sect leading the service in their own way every month. When the Methodists led, the singing would be so good even Aretha's ears might've pricked up. When the Anglican High Church led it was all smells and bells. When the Anglican Low Church led it was flares and jumpers and rainbow strapped guitars. The United Reformists I just wanted to take home and cuddle. They would always do an annoyingly meaningful activity which made me think just how shit a Christian I really was, while the Catholic services were often daunting, led by nuns, their austere faces looking choked by the wimples strapped around them. But it is the Orthodox Church that has perhaps the most different way of worship to the rest of us Christians in the west and they were leading the first gathering of the Federation that academic year; a gathering which, like drinks and canapés in the principal's lodge, was mandatory, but which unlike drinks and canapés in the principal's lodge, I was looking forward to. Always up for seeing how the other half preach, for embracing other ways of life and of being inclusive, I skipped off to the service arm in arm with

Hadrian with all the optimism of Dorothy along the yellow brick road.

But when I saw behind the curtain, the Wizard of Orthodox wasn't all I'd hoped he would be. And having to stand for the entire one-and-a-half-hour duration of the service didn't help that feeling of disappointment.

'I don't know how much longer I can go on,' Hadrian whispered to me.

'How long has it been?' I said shifting about awkwardly.

'Ten minutes.'

'Fuck me. Is that all?'

It wasn't as if you could sing along with the hymns or become absorbed in the story of the sermon to take your mind off your aching legs, since the entire service was conducted in Greek – unless you were Greek, of course, and then I'm sure it would have been a hoot.

Forty minutes in and my feet in wedged boots were on fire, my legs quivering – and not in a good way like they did when Spencer had his head in my crotch.

'I'm going to have to sit down,' I whispered to Hadrian.

'I will if you will,' Hadrian replied.

I looked around to see if anyone else had folded yet, but instead came eye to beady eye with Madeline White.

'Bollocks,' I hissed.

'What?'

'The White Witch is watching.'

But just then redemption came as the presiding clergyman moved before an enormous copper bowl full of holy water – I'd seen smaller paddling pools – and dipped the twig he was holding into it. Once the leaves were soaked, he would tap them three times on the head of each member of the congregation, which approached him in single file down the nave.

'What the fuck is going on?' I said quietly.

'Not a clue, but here we go,' Hadrian said, elbowing me into the line. 'At least we can get the circulation going a bit.'

As we got closer to the front of the queue I realised that the twig the priest was holding was actually more of a branch. And as we got closer still it seemed he was actually brandishing the best part of a small tree, so each member of the congregation looked like they'd done the ice bucket challenge as they returned to their seat.

'Bloody hell,' hissed Hadrian. 'If I wanted to get that wet I'd have had dinner with my ex.'

I wasn't sure if he was referring to the time his angry ex poured a glass of wine over him or the natural lubrication the sight of the annoyingly dishy boyfriend always produced in Hadrian's loins (and mine). Anyway, I had no time to worry about that as I suddenly found myself before the priest, the sprig, twig, branch, whatever it was coming at me like a felled sequoia. He twatted me on the head with it once, twice, but getting wet was suddenly the last thing on my mind because on the third time the branches got caught in my curls.

Oh, for Hadrian's hair! That sacred weapon the priest was wielding would have bounced right off those curls as tight as chain mail, but mine were more Brian May than Roman Emperor and so the more the priest tried to yank it out, the more enmeshed it became. There was still a queue of perhaps a hundred people behind me waiting for a blessing so the priest was keen to get cracking, but his urgency was only slowing things up further and causing me considerable pain as my hair was wrenched from the roots. I tried to explain that, like my belly fat caught in a zip when I try to squeeze into something far too small for me, there was no hurrying things along before they could be separated. This would take patience or possibly some sort of lube. But that was all Greek to him – or rather… anyway, you get the point. All he could see was his beautifully choreographed service in front of the entire Federation going to shit and a whole load of Christians, who were already sick of standing, having to wait even longer for this torture to be over.

So he yanked, one more desperate yank, I clamped my hand over my mouth to stop the inevitable profanity ringing around this sacred place, and finally the branch was free. I scurried back to my pew barely able to see where I was going through watering eyes while Hadrian and the remainder of the flock had to be blessed not only by a branch from an olive tree but a great tuft of wet black curly hair too, which now clung to the holy bough like something pulled from a blocked plughole.

'Bloody ecumenism,' I scowled.

SIX

Hadrian and I were becoming fast friends. We'd often go out clubbing with Richard and Tony – two more in our year group that I would come to look on as brothers – or just stay in our rooms with wine and whine; discussing the lectures we'd endured, bemoaning the pastoral incompetence of the academics in charge of our development as ministers, and generally supporting each other through the trials and tribulations of college life, which can be a testing time for any undergraduate, but when you have the added expectation to be holier than thou day in day out it can be wearing.

'But if you want to be a priest,' I hear you cry, 'you *need* to be holier than thou.'

I beg to differ. Asserting moral superiority over someone is quite the opposite, in my eyes, of what you need to be doing as a minister. If you're called by God to the ministry, then you are called because of who you are, not who some relics of a crusty establishment think you should be.

'I'll drink to that,' said Hadrian as he drained another bottle of white and added it to The Wall Of Shame – the collection of empties that were accumulating on my windowsill and making it resemble an off licence from outside.

'I'm thinking of changing my contraception,' I said, going off topic a little.

Spencer and I were still having regular fun and frankly were more than the fuddies we'd professed to be now. Things were getting serious, but that didn't mean I wanted to get pregnant. On the contrary. In fact I can't bear kids. I'm terrible with them. To this day when I'm in a room with a young parent and their baby, the blood drains from me and I pray for them not to say, 'Would you like to hold her?' And if you wear a dog collar, new mothers and fathers think you are the first person in a room that should hold their precious progeny. 'No!' is what I want to scream, but you can't do that, can you? So I quickly pick up a cup, or a plate, or whatever I can find around me so there's no room for a whingeing child in my arms. That's why if you ever see me at a coffee morning hugging a large potted rubber plant in the corner, there's probably a baby in the room too. But somehow that baby always finds its way into my arms. 'What are you supposed to do with it now?' I'm bursting to say. The usual procedure, as far as I've seen, is to make high pitched 'Oozie-boozie' sounds and smile goofily at it, but I just can't bring myself to do it. I'd rather sit it down and say, 'Baby girl, we need to talk. There's so much you need to know about this screwed up patriarchy you've landed in. In a nutshell, you're fucked.' Perhaps that's why within seconds their bottom lip curls over and they start grizzling. 'Oh no, I think she wants Mummy,' I say hopefully, but Mummy has invariably seized the opportunity for a break from her snivelling dependant and is outside having a vape or a scroll through Instagram. When kids get to the age where you can have a conversation with them, then I have all the time in the world for them, but the idea of having a mewling puking blob of my own was unthinkable.

'What are you on now?' Hadrian asked.

'Red Martini,' I said, holding up my glass for his inspection.

'It's all we've got left,' Tony laughed.

'No!' Hadrian tutted. 'What contraception are you on now?'

'Oh!' I said as, rather than drop, the penny floated down slowly through my booze-addled brain. 'The pill.'

'Isn't that the best option?' Richard said.

'Well, it can make your tits ache, fill your face with spots and if I'm honest I'm just shit at remembering to take it.'

'But isn't it the most reliable?' Tony said, all ears.

'Actually, the coil is even more reliable,' I informed him. 'And you never have to remember to take that, coz it's always there up your fu-fu.'

The boys all crossed their legs involuntarily as they imagined the metal device being inserted, and the next day, after my hangover had waned and I'd cleaned the toilet of the remnants of the red Martini I'd vomited there, I went to the local health centre where the chirpy nurse tried to do just that.

But there was something wrong.

'This hurts,' I said, wincing. 'Is it meant to hurt this much?'

The second nurse in the room, who was rightly and properly there for safeguarding reasons, took my hand. 'You'll be fine,' she cooed. 'It's OK.'

I appreciated her effort, but I hadn't felt this much pain since that Orthodox priest ripped my hair out. In fact it was far more eye-watering than that. And the more painful it got the more I tensed up.

'No,' the nurse said, coming up for air. 'I'm really sorry. I can't seem to get it in. I must be having an off day.'

'I understand. It's Monday, everyone feels rough today,' I said with great empathy, the hangover still pressing at the back of my eyes.

'I don't want to keep trying and making you more uncomfortable, so how about you come back next week and we'll have another stab at it?'

Not the best choice of words, but I knew what she meant.

'And feel free to bring a friend, if it helps,' said the other nurse who had imprints of my nails in her hand. 'It might make you feel more relaxed.'

*

The following week I was back, feet in stirrups, legs spread, the nurse with her head between them and the other nurse eyeing Hadrian suspiciously as he sat holding my hand and cursing in my ear.

'You bloody well owe me one,' he said.

'I know,' I winced.

'This is above and beyond my duties as a friend.'

'I know, I'm sorry, but if I'd told you exactly what we were here for you'd never have come, would you?'

38

'Too right. When they said bring a friend they probably meant a girlfriend. I'm not good with vaginas.'

'You don't have to be. You're not the one putting in the coil. Why are you even looking down there?' I said, gripping his hand tighter.

'It's like a road traffic accident. You know you shouldn't stop and look, but...'

'Just shut up and talk to me, will you?' I growled.

'Shut up *and* talk to you?'

'I mean, talk to me to take my mind off the pain.'

'Oh, yes, sorry. OK. Erm...' He racked his brains for a moment then said, 'Do you know what I'm having for my tea tonight?'

'What?' I frowned.

'A large doner kebab,' he laughed. 'Or perhaps a bacon sarnie.'

'Fuck off!' I said. But I had to laugh too.

However, once again, it seemed the nurse was having an off day.

'I'm going to have to refer you to a specialist because it seems you have quite a unique cervix.'

Hadrian nudged me and gurned an impressed face, as if the nurse had just said I had the lungs of a fifteen-year-old athlete.

'I don't think that's a good thing,' I hissed at him.

'Oh,' he sighed.

So Hadrian and I left the surgery, me feeling ever so tightly wound, and yet most definitely un-coiled.

My appointment with the specialist was ten days later. It was right on the other side of Cambridge, but like every good student in the city I owned a bike so I could cycle there in no time. I'd had a shot before I left to loosen me up and I'd had a Hollywood wax the day before so at least I was sure she wouldn't need a machete to find her way inside.

'Should I be worried?' I asked her before she got stuck in.

'I've been doing this for seventeen years,' said the rather stern looking dame. 'I have a one hundred percent success rate and I'm not about to let that slip now.'

Despite her stony expression, I felt reassured. It was a win-win if she came up trumps. I got loads of safe sex and she maintained her flawless stats.

Forty-five painful minutes later the nurse holding my hand was almost in tears just from watching – Hadrian, needless to say, had not been persuaded to return for a second round of Beat the Vagina – and the specialist was red-faced. I'm sure she had a very lovely bedside manner usually, however, I had just sullied her perfect run.

'I am furious,' she said, pacing the room. 'How can that happen? I'm gutted, completely gutted. You've ruined my score. Seventeen years. Seventeen years and not one failure.'

And somehow I found myself apologising even though it was I who was lying there with my legs in the air in agony.

'The coil is clearly not for you and your strangely shaped cervix,' she snapped. 'You'll have to find another method.' She ripped off her gloves and threw them in the pedal bin, the lid of which whacked against the wall, announcing her departure.

'Bye, then,' I whimpered. 'Er... Thank you.'

A few minutes later I was looking at my bicycle in a whole new way. Instead of the seat I saw an enormous razor blade that I was going to have to grind against for the next half hour. So I rode back standing on the pedals as if I were a twelve-year-old trying to be cool in front of his mates.

When I finally made it to the college my legs were so weak that I soon resolved to crawl across the court, something which I had done plenty of times before but usually after a skinful of booze, which served me right. This time I felt indignant at the injustice of having a fiery fanny and jelly legs through no fault of my own and was muttering something to that effect when I saw a pair of achingly sensible shoes blocking my way. I looked up.

'What on earth are you doing?' said the now all too familiar rasp of the White Witch.

Shit.

'Just overdid it at the gym, that's all,' I smiled. 'Got to keep fit. Mind, body and soul,' I smiled sweetly.

As a good Christian and the person who oversaw my well-being in college, I expected that at any moment she might reach down and help me inside like the good Samaritan.

She sniffed derisively and walked away.

SEVEN

Sniffs of derision aimed at me were not the sole preserve of the White Witch. Some of the more uptight second years – usually the ones who were married with kids and whose vaginas were as cobwebbed as Miss Havisham's dining room – could be snotty. Principal David Tanner too would often look down his inflamed strawberry nose at me at times when our paths crossed.

Well into my first year now, I eagerly skipped across the court to the porter's lodge where the mail was deposited. There in my pigeon hole was an exciting treat. David was in the room at the time and must have heard the little squeal of excitement that slipped out of me.

'Good news?' he said over my shoulder.

'The latest edition of my favourite magazine subscription,' I beamed.

'Oh? Which one?' he peered over his half-moon specs at the cover, no doubt expecting to see *Premier Christianity*. The old dinosaur might have even settled for *Ordained*, despite it being – God forbid! – by women in the ministry for women in the ministry.

'*Vogue*,' I said proudly showing him how fabulous Sienna Miller looked in a gold sparkly halter neck.

His face went even greyer if that were possible and he sniffed one of those derisive sniffs and said, 'I might have known,' as he glided off like the Ghost of Christmases Shat On.

Dear old David, and many of the other fossils in that college, believed that if you enjoyed reading fashion magazines and dressed stylishly in Karen Millen and Jimmy Choo as opposed to brown baggy sweaters and beige cords (and that was just the women), then there couldn't possibly be any room inside that pretty little head of yours for the Bible or theology. Not only were they completely wrong, I often found in lectures that I seemed to know the Bible better than half of the lecturers. I gave them the benefit of the doubt

42

at first, since most of them looked so decrepit that dementia might well have been a factor in their slip-ups, but Dr Price didn't have that excuse. He was barely middle-aged and thought he was very worldly. He would constantly crow about how often he went to Africa to help the *poor black children.*

'Perhaps the poor black children might benefit more if he stopped all these intercontinental flights with their massive carbon footprints,' I whispered to Hadrian, who snorted his appreciation into his notebook.

'Yes?' Dr Price said.

He was looking at me. I pointed to myself.

'Yes, you. You have something to contribute?'

'No, no.'

'Good,' he frowned, eyeing me like Clint Eastwood on the dusty street of a one-horse town for a moment before continuing to harp on about his charitable efforts.

As his course wore on, I wondered if my fellow students had noticed the errors too and were just too polite to say, so I thought I'd get the ball rolling and stuck up my hand.

It turns out that pointing out to Dr Price that he was incorrect to describe Gabriel as an archangel when in the Bible only Michael is described as one, goes down like a cup of cold sick.

I should have known, really. In the very first lecture he took at the beginning of the year, Dr Price's idea of an ice-breaker was to ask each student in the room to say their name, which college they were from and to quote their favourite verses from the Bible, explaining why the passage meant so much to them. The main problem with this, apart from the avalanche of virtue-signalling that was about to be spewed into the room, was that the entire Federation took these lectures together. In our tiny college, this exercise would have lasted a few minutes, but there were more than fifty of us of all denominations in this lecture theatre.

'This is going to be interminable,' I sighed to Hadrian from behind a ring binder.

And so it was.

'Hi, I'm Scott,' said the keeny at the front. 'I'm from Ridley Hall and my favourite passage is John 3:16, *For God so loved the world that he gave his one and only Son, that whoever believes in him shall not perish but have eternal life.* And this passage is so important to me because...' I thought Scott might well up at any moment. '...it is the crux of my ministry, it's why I'm here. Because it's that saving power of Jesus which has brought me to this place...'

I'd already zoned out so I'm not sure if he ever actually got to the point. And he was just the first. Since, like all naughty boys and girls, Hadrian and I were at the back of the room, there were forty more outpourings of pious bullshit before they got to our row and by that time – by the look on Dr Price's face – even he was starting to regret his bright idea. So when it came to me I thought a lightening of the atmosphere was in order. I introduced myself and where I was from and told the room that, 'My favourite Bible passage is from the New International Version of the Bible – it must be that particular translation, mind you – and it's Psalm 56 verse 1.'

'Ah,' Dr Price said, just a little put out because: 'I'm not sure I know that Psalm too well in that particular translation.'

'Well, let me share it with you, because this is a passage that I can relate to only too well.'

He was all ears. As was the rest of the room. 'Go ahead.'

'*Oh Lord, be merciful to me for men hotly pursue me all day long.* Story of my life.'

The words are of course spoken by King David as Saul's soldiers try to hunt him down and murder him. Taken out of context it raised the necessary giggles from some of the audience, but Dr Price chuckled as one of his *poor black children* might, having queued for an hour in the burning sun for a handful of milk powder.

But that's the thing with the Bible. You can pretty much make it mean anything you like. That's how Christians justified slavery for so many years, how women have been

44

shat on since the first word was written, and of course why all homosexuals are going to hell. (They're not, by the way; they're fabulous just as they are). Playing Bible ping pong as a liberal lefty with right-wing evangelicals became a sport for me. Whatever they spat out that justified discrimination I came back with an inclusive quote from Jesus, usually with a side order of: 'If you take the Bible that literally, why haven't you sold everything you have and given it to the poor yet?'

Apart from the odd factual clanger in class, I was more concerned that Dr Price, among others, seemed never to question the misogyny inherent in the Bible and the cultures it depicts, even though it is clearly rife with it. You don't have to read more than a few pages before the first example: Adam and Eve. Eve is created from a piece of Adam – or in other words, without Adam there would be no Eve. And she's only created to please the poor old lonely bloke. Well, he'd go blind if he was left to his own devices much longer, wouldn't he? I like to think she was really brought into the picture because Adam was inept and someone needed to get shit done around Eden. But we are led to believe that it is Eve who was the weak one. She's the one who was tempted to eat from the Tree of Knowledge, although Adam probably neglected to tell her that it was forbidden, just as he probably neglected to tell her that he was going out for a drink after work. By having her ruin Eden for both of them, for us all, the male concoctors of this story set women up from day one to take the blame for anything that sucks.

Leviticus tells us that the Lord told Moses, '*A woman who becomes pregnant and gives birth to a son will be ceremonially unclean for seven days, just as she is unclean during her monthly period. On the eighth day the boy is to be circumcised. Then the woman must wait thirty-three days to be purified from her bleeding. She must not touch anything sacred or go to the sanctuary until the days of her purification are over.*' And this may come as no surprise: '*If she gives birth to a* daughter, *for two weeks the woman will be unclean, as during her period. Then she must wait sixty-*

six days to be purified from her bleeding.' Double penance for having a *mere* girl!

If only men had periods they would probably argue that only men could possibly be priests because their sins are physically being washed away by the bleeding. They would brag about the size of their tampons, which would be free on the NHS of course, and they'd get paid leave from their jobs every month so they could endure the discomfort of menstruating in the comfort of their homes while they'd crow about such a sacred thing happening to their bodies.

In the Bible the female body is often seen as dangerous, unclean, and a source of potential contamination. In the book of Isaiah women are seen as vain and obsessed with their appearance:

The women of Zion are haughty, walking along with outstretched necks, flirting with their eyes, strutting along with swaying hips, with ornaments jingling on their ankles.

They sound like the beauties I might admire in *Vogue*, and yet apparently the Lord will bring sores on their heads and:

Instead of fragrance there will be a stench; instead of a sash, a rope; instead of well-dressed hair, baldness; instead of fine clothing, sackcloth; instead of beauty, branding.

Seems a bit harsh. But then, we all know women need to learn to dress down otherwise they're asking to be raped. Don't we?

With all this in mind, I couldn't hold my tongue any longer when Dr Price was talking about the gospel of Saint John one day – Chapter 8, to be precise – in which the teachers of law dragged a woman before Jesus and said words to the effect of, 'This slapper was caught in the act of adultery. The law commands us to stone such tarts. What say you?' That's when Jesus uttered the pretty cool line, 'Let any of you who is without sin cast the first stone.' And so they all sloped off.

'Yes,' Dr Price said impatiently when he saw my hand was raised.

46

'Do you think it's telling that we never hear from the woman herself during all this? She is not allowed to defend herself or tell her side of the story. She could have been raped for all we know because in the case of an engaged or married woman, the law did not differentiate between rape and adultery; she would have been executed in either case. And where's the bloke she committed this *adultery* with? I notice he doesn't get a good stoning. Isn't this all a prime example of the misogyny inherent in Bible law?'

I felt the air go cold. I felt Hadrian's nails digging into my hand just as mine had done to his when I was legs akimbo having the coil unsuccessfully rammed up into me. I'm not sure if he was trying to tell me to shut up or if he was holding on for dear life as he waited for Dr Price to explode.

Long minutes seemed to pass as Dr Price composed a no doubt eloquent response. Then he sniffed, one of those derisive sniffs – is there a cold going round? – and carried on with his well-worn spiel as if I'd never said a word. Just like the woman in the temple courts, it seemed I was voiceless.

EIGHT

To recover from that lecture, Hadrian and I went to the bar over the road for a couple of stiff ones. In fact the bar was full of stiff ones, belonging as it did to the college.

'Well, that was depressing,' I said as I ordered a couple of G and Ts.

'That was nothing,' Hadrian groaned, leaning on the bar.

'What do you mean?'

'On Sunday I was sent to North London.'

We were often sent out to churches all over the place to preach as part of our training, so this wasn't huge news to me.

'Sounds grim,' I offered supportively, not being a fan of the Big Smoke either.

'It's not. I love London,' Hadrian said. 'Where else can I walk hand in hand down the street with another boy and nobody bats a false eyelash? It's a cultural melting pot. All creeds and colours.'

'True,' I nodded over the rim of my glass, leaning on the bar too.

Hadrian continued, 'So I was quite excited when I found myself in a black church. It was my first time in one. They always seem to have more fun in their services and the music is much better.'

'Was Dr Price there,' I said wryly, 'handing out food parcels?'

'But I hadn't really reworked my address,' Hadrian went on. 'I didn't have time with all the essays coming out of my ears. I'd used it in other churches, so I thought I'd just rehash it yet again. I didn't even think about the language until I opened my stupid gob and heard myself saying, *The blood of Christ washes us clean of the darkness of sin, making us as pure and as white as snow.*'

I nearly spat my Tanqueray and tonic across the bar.

'So I quickly flicked to another page in the Bible where I knew sin was mentioned to try and cover my tracks. 1 John, I told myself. 1 John, Chapter 1, verse 9.'

'You mean,' I said, reciting the passage for him, '*Lord Jesus, let nothing unholy remain, Apply Thine own blood and extract every stain; To get this blest cleansing, I all things forego, Now wash me, and I shall be whiter than snow.*'

Hadrian nodded mournfully.

'Oh dear.'

'Oh dear? That's an understatement,' he cried. 'So I flicked through to Isaiah 1:18. *Come now, let us settle the matter, says the Lord. Though your sins are like scarlet, they shall be as white as snow; though they are red as crimson, they shall be like wool.*'

'The previous verse being, if I remember rightly,' I added, '*Learn to do right; seek justice and correct the oppressor.*'

'Exactly,' he cringed at the irony. 'The fucking Bible is...' he searched for the words.

I assisted: '... a crock of shite.'

He nodded into his drink.

'That's what I was trying to point out to Dr Price,' I said. 'It's a relic. Outdated. Written by men with an agenda thousands of years ago in a language that's dead.'

Don't get me wrong, the Bible has some brilliant, powerful moments, but then so did *EastEnders* back in the day.

Talking of outdated, just then I felt a hand slip up my stockinged thigh heading towards my crotch. I straightened up and spun round. 'What the fuck?' I snapped at Piers, another first year, also from our college.

'Come on,' he slurred, 'give us a go!'

'A go?' I said. 'What am I, a PlayStation?'

'Well, I've got the joystick, baby.'

'In your dreams, pal,' I growled.

'Come on, you know you want to.'

I sighed. 'You could finger me, Piers, if you were 1) attractive, 2) had fingers that didn't resemble twiglets, 3) had a penis more impressive than a grape and 4) and listen carefully as this is the most important one: had my *permission*. But since you don't have any of those things, what makes you think you have the right to touch me anywhere, let alone try to fucking finger me?'

Piers tutted. 'You were there bending over in your little skirt.'

'I was here having a drink, leaning on the bar wearing what I choose to wear, which is my right and none of your fucking business.'

'Ooooh,' he said, miming clutching a handbag to his chest – a stock male non-response to a woman who calls them out on their bullshit. 'Might have known.'

'Might have known what?'

'All this feminist crap.'

'Hadrian, stop me before I punch him!' I muttered, loud enough so Piers could hear.

Hadrian looked him up and down with disgust and clearly no intention of stopping me if I really did lay him out.

'I heard you in the lecture,' Piers sneered, 'siding with the tart in the temple.'

'What translation did you read to find out she was a *tart* and what exactly do you mean by that offensive term?'

'She was an adulterer.'

'OK, let's murder all adulterers! Everyone get in line behind Prince Charles and Bill Clinton! Piers, did you not hear what I said in there? She could have been raped. But yes, let's say she'd had an affair. Probably because her husband was a dick,' I said pointedly at the dick before me. 'Or because she was forced into marriage. Perhaps her husband died and, as you know, it was Levitical law for a woman to then marry her deceased husband's brother and bear his children without a bloody say. Perhaps actually she really fancies the bloke next door, but she won't get a say in what happens to her, will she? People have affairs all the time, Piers. When *you're* a priest – God help us! – you might need to minister to someone who needs your guidance through a rocky relationship. Perhaps a woman for whom things have got complicated, messy, even. Then what will you do?'

'Fuck her till she bleeds, which is what I'd like to do to you.'

'Where's the White Witch when you actually need her?' I sighed and went back to my drink. He was offensive and disgusting, but best ignored. Like a zit, picking at it would only make it worse. And so Piers slithered away.

A few hours later Hadrian and I thought we'd better get back to our rooms and catch up on some reading. He went off to the toilet first, while I made my way to the exit, where I was accosted by a very mature student we affectionately called Father Jack (after the old alcoholic from *Father Ted*).

'I thought you were amazing earlier. Standing up to that little prick Piers.'

'Why thank you...' I began but was struck dumb by Father Jack putting his hands on my breasts.

'I just really want to... really let you know...' He puckered up and leaned in. His breath was as fragrant as landfill. And yet, even if it had tasted of ambrosia I would have knocked the letch back.

I quickly found my voice again. 'What are you doing?' And I laughed at the codger since he posed no real threat, turned him around and pushed him away.

Father Jack stumbled off grumbling something about women and I invited Hadrian in for a drink at mine as we left.

'I thought we were catching up on reading,' he said. 'Are you OK?'

He could see I was preoccupied with something and, like the great minister he would one day be, he lent an ear.

'I can laugh off Father Jack, I can kick Piers and little pricks like him into shape, but why the hell should I have to? Why do I have to dress down to avoid being groped?'

Hadrian nodded sympathetically. 'It starts in schools. Girls are told to dress like Victorians so that boys don't have to learn self-control.'

'When we get out in the real world and minister for real,' I said, 'we have to be real too, not Biblical anachronisms like these relics that run this place would have us be. OK?'

'Deal,' Hadrian said and we drank to that.

It wasn't long before Tony and Richard sniffed a session in the making and stopped by with wine to whine. By 2 a.m. we had put the ecclesiastical world to rights and drunk our rooms dry.

'Shit,' I said, staring at my windowsill. 'The Wall of Shame is too full. It's time it was emptied.'

NINE

There was a large recycling dumpster in a gated alcove on the other side of the college where bottles and the like were supposed to be disposed of, but I figured that walking across the court in broad daylight with shopping bags bursting with empty booze bottles would do nothing to heal that epidemic that was going around, the main symptoms of which were a sniff and a judgement. What's more, since the windowsill currently looked like an outlet of Majestic I would have to do at least three trips on my own, maximizing the possibility of being frowned upon. So I decided that, cloaked in the night, Hadrian, Tony, Richard and I could steal across the court together and dump the entire Wall of Shame in one foul swoop without anyone noticing.

I might have recalled that the last time I had a big idea in the wee small hours after plenty of fortified grape juice was at Spencer's party when he caught me searching for porn under his bed. And perhaps my cloudy brain did at some point recall that, but instead of the memory corroborating the theory that our common sense is impaired somewhat after drinking, I must have used it as an example of just how such decision making can result in great things – after all, Spencer and I were now together and as happy as Adam and Eve before the fall... the fall, which was of course blamed on Eve by the patriarchy, who painted her as a temptress leading her husband into religious deviancy, salvation from which is only to be found, if you believe their bollocks, in a celibate Christ born into the world by a virgin, an unsullied foil to Eve... And thus my Cinzano'd brain went on, until I found four Tesco bags under the sink and handed them out to each of my lovely brothers.

We proceeded to fill the bags with the empty bottles, which clanged together so loudly in our uncoordinated hands that it must have sounded like the bell ringing club were rehearsing in my room, so I told everyone just that in an effort to keep us all quiet.

'Campanology,' said Hadrian.

'What's that?' said Tony, 'The science of being Hadrian?' and he minced about the room as was Hadrian's wont from time to time.

'No, you dick,' Hadrian laughed, throwing a cushion at him. 'Bell ringing. The proper name for it is campanology.'

'I know that,' Tony said. 'We do the classics too. Campana is Latin for bell.'

'Logia, Greek for the study of,' Richard added.

I winced at the thought of being in Greek lessons where conjugated verbs came at me like the headlights of a juggernaut. 'Let's not talk about Greek right now. I might bring up the Advocaat.' Yes, things had got so desperate that I had been reduced to draining the bottle that stays in the back of every cupboard eternally, only to make a brief appearance at Christmas as a poor substitute for proper eggnog. It was November.

'Give me more bottles!' Hadrian whisper-shouted. 'I have loads of room in here.'

I shushed Hadrian and then he shushed me and then we all shushed each other louder than the clanging of the bottles, but somehow we were soon ready for action.

We slipped as stealthily as foxes might – if they were wearing hobnail boots, the soles covered in tar – down the stairs and out into the cold night air. Then, Tesco bags clutched to our chests, we tiptoed from bush to bush.

'We're like four James Bonds,' Hadrian giggled.

'Which one are you?' Richard asked him.

'Brosnan of course. He always had a twinkle in his eye.'

'I'm Connery,' Tony said.

'No, I'm Connery,' Richard argued.

'Well, I'm M,' I hissed, 'and I order you to shut the fuck up!'

Hadrian giggled even more, but somehow we made it to the gate without the court being flooded with light from the bedrooms of disturbed students and tutors.

'Shit,' I heard from the shadows.

'What?'

'The gate's locked.' Tony tutted.

'Who would lock a gate to a dumpster?' Hadrian cried. 'I mean, what did they think someone would do, steal it?'

'It's probably to discourage idiots from coming out at two in the morning and making a racket,' I said sarcastically.

'Oh yeah,' Hadrian nodded.

This is the point where sober, sensible and frankly very dull people would go home to bed.

'OK. One of us has to go over the top,' I said.

'You,' the boys chorused at me.

'Me?' I squeaked. 'I'm in a skirt.'

'You've got knickers on, haven't you?' Tony said.

'Yes.'

'Makes a change,' Hadrian sniggered.

'Fuck off,' I smirked.

'So what's the problem?' Richard sighed.

'You're the smallest,' Hadrian slurred.

'And the lightest,' Richard added. 'We can't lift anyone else.'

'And they're your bloody bottles,' Tony concluded.

Their reasoning was sound to my sloshed self and within seconds I found myself getting a leg up and almost impaling myself on one of the vertical slats that constituted the gate.

'Bloody hell,' I gasped. 'Someone come round and help me down the other side!'

'If we could do that you wouldn't have to climb over in the first place, you nugget,' Hadrian called up.

'Oh yeah,' I said and so I jumped off the gate and landed on the floor whacking the dumpster with my hands to steady myself, which sounded like a bass drum.

We all froze and listened for a moment for the sound of the porter or an angry tutor approaching.

Nothing.

When Tony gave the all clear, the boys passed the Tesco bags over the gate and I proceeded to pour the bottles into the dumpster. It was a Niagara Falls of glass.

'Just lower the bags in!' Richard cried.

'No. I want them back. It's important to reuse,' I said. 'I'm dating a pilot. Got to offset the carbon footprint somehow.'

'It's too much noise. You have to…' he began.

'RUN!' I heard someone say followed by three pairs of boy's shoes scampering off into the night.

I slipped into the shadows by the dumpster as a light from the lodge next door flooded the ground outside the gate and from the lodge came its resident: the White Witch.

Madeline White, in a stripy pyjama set worthy of a seventies sitcom, appeared by the gate, hands on hips looking about the court. Then she turned an eye to the gate and looked through the slats just as the T-Rex did through the window of the jeep on *Jurassic Park*, looking for prey to devour. For what seemed like the entire Jurassic and Cretaceous period combined I held my breath as the reptilian eye scanned the alcove. I scrunched up my eyes in an effort to disappear, convinced the witch could smell me even if she couldn't see me. But at last, satisfied that the perpetrators had scarpered, she huffed, her breath like dragon smoke in the November air and retreated back into her lair.

For fear of being spotted I would have stayed there for the rest of the night, but I wasn't really dressed for the weather. So when I was as sure as I could be that Madeline was fast asleep again, I clambered up onto the dumpster, along the wall and back onto the gate where I dropped down with more grace this time, and without the three James Bonds to draw attention to me, I slinked back to my room, to my bed, and slept fitfully, dreaming of dinosaurs shouting in Greek and throwing bells at me.

TEN

One day in December I scurried across the frosty court to the porter's lodge to see if the latest edition of *Vogue* had arrived. It hadn't yet, but there was an envelope in my pigeon hole. No stamp. It was an internal missive. And it was sealed with sticky tape as if the contents were of a highly sensitive nature which no one else should be privy to. However, inside was simply a letter from the principal inviting me to meet him in his office on Tuesday morning at 10 a.m. But it also stated that whatever lecture or appointment I might have at that time, this meeting was to take priority. It was clearly more of an order than an invitation and it began to unsettle me. I was convinced this was not going to be a good meeting, so, ensconced in a Starbucks, coz it was warmer than our rooms, warming our hands on skinny lattes, I showed the letter to Hadrian just in case I was being neurotic.

'Shit,' he sang.

So I guess I wasn't.

'What have you done to piss off David?'

'Nothing,' I said immediately, but then after pondering hard on the question, 'Oh no!'

'What?' Hadrian sat up as if a guy had just walked on set on the *Jerry Springer Show* to find his girlfriend was now a man, or a sheep, or whatever other nonsense those rednecks got themselves into.

'I wonder if he found the knickers.'

'The what?' Hadrian was on the edge of his seat now.

'My knickers. Before the service on the first day of term, Spencer and I had been going at it and then I heard the bell and I rushed over to the chapel...'

'I remember you walking in last and I thought, who's that little slut?'

'Hadrian!'

'Then I thought, nice shoes.'

'Ah thanks, love.' I relished the compliment for a moment before remembering what we were talking about. 'Anyway. I leaked jizz into my knickers and then we had to go straight to David's lodge for canapés, remember? And then I was all soggy so I went to his bathroom and took my knickers off to dry them, but I couldn't do it properly so I decided just to get rid of them and I threw them in his bin.'

Hadrian nearly choked on his coffee.

'You OK, love?'

'Oh yeah,' he said, tapping at his chest. 'Not the first time something hot and milky went down the wrong way.' He focused on me again through his watering eyes. 'Your knickers?'

I nodded. 'They were Victoria's Secret as well.'

'Oh, nice.' Hadrian was genuinely interested. 'Lacy?'

I nodded. 'Black.'

Hadrian gurned his approval, but we were getting off topic again.

So I said, 'But what if he found them?'

'Then the dirty old bastard would probably be tossing himself off over them every time his wife was out. He wouldn't be admitting to anyone he found them.'

'His wife!' I cried. 'What if Charlotte found them?'

'Then she'd probably be filing for divorce right now. Why would you get into trouble for that? Your mum didn't sew your name into them so they didn't get mixed up in the changing rooms, did she?'

'Of course not,' I scoffed.

'So how would anyone know they were yours?'

I sighed a huge sigh of relief and thanked God for Hadrian, the voice of reason as I knew he would be. 'But why does he want to see me, then?'

'Could it be when you had a fight with the priest at the Orthodox Church service?'

'It wasn't my fault my hair got caught up in his bloody big branch thing. He should be apologising to me for that. It hurt. Besides, that was ages ago now.'

'Mmmm,' Hadrian mused.

'The White Witch might have said something when I came back from that failed coil fitting and she found me crawling across the grass.'

'Well, your fanny was aflame, darling, it couldn't be helped.'

'*We* know that,' I agreed, 'but funnily enough I didn't share that with Madeline.'

'She *is* your personal tutor. You should be able to share personal things with her,' he grinned.

'Not helping,' I scowled.

'Sorry,' Hadrian smothered his smile. 'OK. So let's think!'

And so we did. And after a moment or two Hadrian declared, 'The Wall of Shame.'

'The recycling dumpster,' I added. 'She must have seen me in there or running away or... Oh no.'

'Why didn't we all get letters then? Me, Tony, Richard.'

'Because you buggered off and left me, you bastards.'

'Yes, sorry about that,' Hadrian said softly, remorsefully. 'Forgive me?'

'Of course I forgive you, mate,' I said, putting my hand gently on his knee. 'I would have buggered off too if you had been the one at the dumpster.'

'Oh thanks.' He pantomimed indignation.

'OK,' I said formulating my response to David, 'it's bound to be that. I'll just explain that I had a lot of bottles to get rid of and I wanted to do it discreetly. So I thought 2 a.m. would be the most discreet time, but I hadn't bargained for the gate being locked.'

'Perhaps it's the number of bottles that David or Madeline have a problem with.'

'I bet David has crates full of empty bottles of shit red wine from all his soirées. Mine only accumulated, I'll tell him, because I was studying so hard I didn't have time to recycle them. I bet he has a maid or something to empty his bins.'

'Perhaps the maid saw the knickers then,' Hadrian smiled.

'Don't start that again!' I slapped his arm. 'I'm paranoid enough as it is.'

ELEVEN

And so Tuesday came and for once I wished I was in Dr Price's lecture instead of traipsing with all the velocity of a snail unwillingly to David Tanner's lodge.

When he showed me through to his enormous study, the tome-lined room where I'd had canapés and moist underwear on that first night of term, I shuddered to see Madeline White sitting there on David's side of the huge mahogany desk, on a green leather chair, the twin of the one David now settled in, except I think hers was trimmed with icicles and perhaps there was the pelt of a polar bear draped over it too. I was directed to sit on the other side of the desk in a chair to rival the Van Gogh one in my room for comfort, though, unlike mine, it seemed to have been made by and for Oompa Loompas. David had set the scene perfectly to affirm his great white male position of power over me. I felt suitably inferior. But I was ready to explain my bottle collection and my badly timed recycling trip.

'OK, splendid,' David said when we were all settled, or unsettled in my case. I wasn't sure what was splendid about any of this, but I didn't argue that point. 'I'm afraid, my dear, there's been some complaints made against you.'

'Oh?' I said looking at Madeline.

'Yes. From other members of the college,' David said.

So, not Madeline, I thought. It seemed this might not be about empty booze bottles after all. But if it wasn't, what on earth could it be about?

'Your behaviour has been rather inappropriate,' David went on.

Inappropriate? I thought of the headboard on my bed which still regularly announced to all and sundry that I was enjoying a good rogering from Spencer. We'd tried to move the bed away from the wall, but it continued to creak like the Mary Rose in a storm. I mean, what's a budding priest supposed to do, be celibate? I suppose the nuns in the Federation might have something to say about that, but I wasn't a nun and… David was talking. I focused with all my might.

'So we're not quite sure if you're fit for ministry.' He looked over his glasses sternly at me.

'Um…' I was betwattled. 'Why?' I said weakly.

'Your behaviour in classes also leaves a lot to be desired.'

'Really?' I said, my voice trembling a little. 'But I get involved in classes. I ask questions and I answer questions as often as I can. What is it that I'm doing wrong exactly?'

'I think if you take the time during the Christmas vacation to reflect on your behaviour over this last term you will be able to answer that for yourself. This is a very serious situation, but,' he said as if he were doing me a favour, 'we will treat this informally for now.'

'But you mentioned inappropriate behaviour,' I said, sensing I was about to be dismissed without an answer. 'What did I do that was inappropriate?'

David seemed to redden a little and looked to Madeline, who didn't seem to want to take the sticky baton from him.

'That's all for now,' David said.

'But what did…?'

'When you come back next term we can discuss a way forward. Go and reflect!' he said, looking almost as nervous as I felt. 'You know what you have done.'

And that was it. I was dismissed and spent the vacation in turmoil knowing my future was in jeopardy but not knowing why. I spent sleepless nights retracing my steps and my actions in college and recalling my words in classes. I worked out my frustrations in the gym with a Rihanna song blasting in my ears, the lyrics telling me to just live my life while David's voice battled with it telling me to do nothing of the sort. I prayed to God for guidance, but the lightbulb moment David insisted I would have never manifested. My misdemeanours remained a mystery.

TWELVE

The first day of the spring term came with the usual opening service. Spencer was away working so I was most definitely jizz free, Hallelujah! I was bang on time for the service and on my best behaviour. I had to show willing. Had to show David and Madeline that I was, quite literally, singing from the same hymn sheet as everyone else. Canapés in the principal's lodge was more painful for me than ever, but I didn't dare miss it. I stood around making polite conversation and nodding, my brow furrowed with fake accord as Dr Price went on about the mission he had undertaken to Rwanda over the vacation. When Charlotte came bowling over to us, I instinctively cowered, like everyone else, but I did so because I was convinced she would be as disgusted with whatever I had done as her husband was after he'd told her over dinner one evening – I had a feeling something as new-fangled as confidentiality would not be held in high esteem in the Tanner household. But for now no fire nor brimstone rained down on me from her formidable being.

'Who did you go with?' one of the first years was asking Dr Price, his tongue virtually hanging out of his mouth, 'I would love to go too.'

'NFI,' Dr Price said nonchalantly.

'Oh yes, yes, I read about them,' the first year fawned.

'What do you think of the NFI positioning itself as a neo-charismatic fellowship?' said a second year studiously.

And suddenly they were all off. It was NFI this and NFI that and what do you think of the NFI doing blah blah blah and I wanted to stab myself with a breadstick. It was that or make my excuses and slope off. However, just then I felt Charlotte looking at me, that twinkle in her eye and that tight unforgiving mouth. I was suddenly aware of my silence and I convinced myself that unless I did, and quickly, it would get back to David and Madeline that I was not contributing. The only trouble was, I didn't have the foggiest what NFI stood for.

Well, that's a good place to start, I told myself. I bet half the people standing around here have no idea either, but just haven't got the guts to admit it, so I grasped the nettle and piped up, 'Excuse me, I've forgotten exactly what the NFI is. I mean, I know what it is of course,' I lied, 'but I was just wondering, you know, what the initials NFI actually stand for. Just to be specific, I mean...'

Dr Price opened his mouth to avail me of his wisdom, but Charlotte beat him to it.

'Not Fucking Interesting,' she said at the top of her voice before gliding away.

As she went my eyes followed her. I was shocked, but it was the most welcome shock I could remember. And as she went, she turned to me and threw me a smile. The first I had ever seen from her – the first anyone had. She tossed it to me like a bone to a dog and I buried it in my heart with all my other treasured possessions.

*

The next day, convinced that his wife was a kindred spirit and not one of my detractors, I was back in the principal's office with a glimmer of hope; a feeling that was further fed by the fact that it was just him and me this time – Madeline must have been off somewhere on her sleigh grooming a troubled evacuee with Turkish Delight.

'So,' he began. And finished.

And after a painful pause I realised this was the moment when I was supposed to declare the findings of my reflections and tell him what he apparently already knew.

'I'm sorry, David, but I still have no idea what I am being accused of. If you could be really specific about the inappropriate things I have done, then maybe I can make amends.'

David tried to maintain his stern countenance, but I could see he was the one who was uncomfortable now.

He sighed. 'You'll... um... have to go and um... see your personal tutor about that.' And that was all he had to say on the matter.

He ushered me from his office and as I fumbled my way to the front door the way seemed unusually dark. Perhaps it was just my own sense of foreboding after this strange meeting, but I glanced over my shoulder anyway, feeling bizarrely compelled to see if something was blocking the light from the window, and as I left the lodge I was sure I saw Charlotte at the end of the corridor, just standing there, listening, watching.

Whatever or whomever it was, I now found myself out in the cold literally and metaphorically. I couldn't stand any more of this – the metaphorical cold that is. The literal cold was all right. I don't mind winter; it means you can wear some great layered outfits, perhaps a knee-length boot, hats and even a bit of faux fur. But right now I didn't give a shit about all that. I stomped across to Madeline's residence and rapped on her door.

She took her time to open it and when she did she looked offended as I didn't have an appointment – that or she had Edmund Pevensie tied up in the back and was keen to get back to interrogating him.

'Please will you tell me exactly what I've done that's inappropriate? I need specific examples if I am to do anything about it.'

Now she looked less offended and more like me when I was faced with Greek verbs to conjugate.

'You need to go and talk to David about that,' she muttered.

'But he just said…'

She shut the door on me.

I felt like I was the butt of a really cruel prank which had gone on far too long, so I hightailed it back to the principal's lodge and knocked on his door.

'I cannot discuss it. You must ask Madeline!' he said looking so red in the face I wondered if, without my knowing, my mum *had* in fact sewn my name into my knickers after all.

I had a sense of what Mary must have felt like as yet another door was shut in her face. No room at the inn. So there I was again knocking on Madeline White's door.

'David insists you tell me,' I said. 'I need to know, Madeline. This is making me ill now.'

Madeline looked up and down the court as if I had just asked her to sell me a gram or two of cocaine and ushered me inside. Her face was as red as David's had been as we stood in the hallway, no invitation to sit down and counsel me like a – oh, I don't know – personal tutor might. I could tell this was going to be brief.

Madeline shifted about uneasily as she tried to find the words with all the difficulty of someone hacking up a particularly stubborn bit of phlegm. 'You told someone....'

I nodded eagerly, coaxing the words out of her.

'You told them that...'

Oh, sweet baby Jesus, please help her spit it out!

It was as if I had asked her to tell me the details of how she masturbates. She took a deep breath, squirmed, nay, writhed, but finally it came tumbling out. '...that her breasts looked nice in a top she was wearing.' She exhaled like a new mother in the delivery room, as if it had been that much of an effort to say the word *breasts*.

My face stretched in an effort to ask without actually saying, 'Is that *it*?'

'And,' Madeline said loudly, now the floodgates were open, 'you said another student's bo— bottom looked nice in what she was wearing.'

'*AND?*' I wanted to scream. I mean, it's not as if I said, 'You look great for your age.' Or, 'Did you lose weight?' Or, 'You look so good I didn't recognise you.' I had dished out a couple of compliments to women who frankly looked as if they needed some.

'If another woman told me my boobs looked great in a top or my arse looked great in a pair of jeans I'd be over the moon,' I said to Madeline, who was in no danger of ever being on the receiving end of one of my 'offensive' compliments.

'Well,' she brushed off my argument, 'that's just one thing. Your behaviour in class is also inappropriate.'

'I never told Dr Price his package looked good.'

Madeline closed her eyes. 'You are contrary in class. You are overbearing. You want to take control and it seems you are not aware of how that affects others.'

At last, we were getting to the real problem. Dr Price and the other tutors I'd corrected or challenged politely and, I thought, intelligently on the many issues we all should have with the Bible – its misogyny for one – saw my efforts as contrary and overbearing. But is it *taking control* to wake up every student in a room to the fact that they're accepting errors and buying into the patriarchy? Is it overbearing to lighten the mood a bit when the tutor is so beige in his teaching style that every student will doze through his lectures and learn nothing?

Perhaps.

Perhaps I did cross lines now and then, but without the crossing of lines we would still be stuck in the dark ages. Jesus himself crossed lines in order to lead us from ignorance. His mother Mary talked of a Lord who has *scattered those who are proud in their inmost thoughts* and who has *brought down rulers from their thrones but has lifted up the humble.*

Mary was a strong figure who stood by her son at times of great danger and proclaimed that radical message of social justice. But by making her impossibly a virgin the patriarchy was able to create an ideal of womanhood that would universalise guilt among women. The married virgin deprives women of a model of leadership and courage who is also capable of sexual desire and passion. The ever-Virgin diminishes women's sexuality and makes the female body and female sexuality seem unwholesome, impure.

Women are constantly diminished and excluded in the Bible and, it seemed to me, the culture which promoted that was alive and well in the theological colleges of Cambridge, if not the world. And what saddened me the most was that Madeline, who was ostensibly a woman, could not see that.

I wondered: if it was a male student who was the most forward in class, who was questioning, thoughtful and witty, would they be seen as overbearing, challenging and controlling? I had a feeling they wouldn't. No, it was more than a feeling. I knew they wouldn't. We all knew they wouldn't.

Piers could go around with impunity sticking his hands up women's skirts and announcing how he'd like to fuck them till they bled, but should I compliment a fellow woman on her appearance, I am seen as inappropriate. In fact, if I was a married man, breeding, behaving like Piers in the bars and behaving like me in classes, I would find myself climbing the ranks of the church in no time. I know this because it was and is all around me.

I was told I would have to go on a course to learn how to toe the line; how to be a wallflower, a shrinking violet, and generally know my place – yes, there is an actual course for that. And, if I didn't want to get kicked out of the church forever, I had to sign up for it immediately.

If someone suggested that to me nowadays, I would of course tell them where to shove it. I would say, 'How dare you suggest I change who I am and alter my personality to fit your outmoded mouldy mould!' But at that moment I was scared. Scared I would lose my chance to become a minister forever. And scared of the establishment looming over me, which is of course, exactly how it manages to persist. I recalled David's declaration that despite the apparent seriousness of the situation he was going to do me the favour of treating it informally. And yet the consequences were formal.

I'd been shafted.

In fact, if it had been treated formally from that first ridiculous meeting in December, then I would have had rights in that process. The right to representation, the right to have everything documented, and of course David and

Madeline knew that, which is why they didn't do it, because on paper the whole thing would have looked absurd and no formal sanctions could have been applied.

Apart from the course on how to kiss arse, I was ordered to complete an extra year in college. While Hadrian, Richard, Tony and all the rest would be flying off into the big wide world after the second year I was condemned to another year, as if I was doing time in prison until I learnt to be a good girl and shut the fuck up.

In my despair I made an appointment to see a member of the Ministerial Candidates' and Probationers' Oversight Committee to plead for help. They politely said there was nothing they could do when in fact I could see they too were scared; scared to put their own heads above the parapet.

In times gone past, after a nerve-wracking meeting with the McPoc I'd be inclined to stuff my face with a McVeggie burger or two, but I had seriously lost my appetite to the point where, as I felt the college's controlling grip tightening on every part of my existence, I became anorexic.

With hindsight and a lot of self-reflection I know now that I was controlling the only thing the establishment couldn't: what I ate. I dieted dangerously and exercised furiously. The weight dropped off to the point where my bones protruded, my skin was a mess and my periods eventually ceased, but no one in authority, least of all my personal tutor, noticed or did anything about this very personal and worrying change in me. They are ministers, for fuck's sake. Pastoral care is integral to what they do. Or it should be. I had none from them. Like most self-abuse, my eating disorder was a cry for help, but it fell on deaf ears. Yet, even if they had come and shown concern for my weight, encouraged me to eat more, I would have told them where to go, because that was the one thing they couldn't make me do.

*

Amy had joined the college as an undergraduate halfway through the first year. She must have noticed how the compulsory communal meal once a week stressed me out –

the idea of eating in front of anyone is often anathema to someone with an eating disorder.

'Will you come and have dinner with me?' she asked one day.

I must have looked like Madeline White did when she had to say *breasts* to me.

'I'm not going to cook for you,' Amy said softly. 'You bring whatever you're comfortable eating. Doesn't matter what it is. How much. How little. You do you and I'll do me. But we'll be together.'

Now that's a minister. Kind and gentle and so supportive.

As my skin deteriorated, eczema flared up on my back so severely that I could barely wear clothes without pain. But Amy was there to apply ointment to my skin. Those tender moments conjured up images of the woman in the Bible who came to anoint Jesus's feet and in a great display of humility dried them with her own hair. The identity of this woman is the source of some contention, because – yet again – this woman, as so many are in the Bible, is described as a *sinner*. Christians have an historical tendency to interpret a non-specified sin in women of the Bible as sexual sin, and often, female promiscuity is inferred with no support from the actual text. It is likely that this woman was in fact no such sinner but the sister of Lazarus whose only sin was to confront Jesus for not being there to save her brother. He would of course go on to resurrect Lazarus, hence his sister's repentant act at Jesus's feet. And she would even be there again to anoint his body after the crucifixion.

How quickly men unjustly heap shame on women in the Bible. How quickly men unjustly heap shame on women in the world. I felt shame now too, but thank God for people like Amy who helped me hold onto hope.

THIRTEEN

Then there were the bruises.

One morning, Spencer lifted his head up from between my legs – he didn't sleep there, although with tongue action like his, I probably wouldn't have minded if he did – and said, 'Babe, you're black and blue. What the hell's going on?'

He had spotted the marks on my inner thighs and my shins. I hid my face in the pillow as if I was still sleepy. 'It's nothing,' I said through a mouthful of hypoallergenic memory foam.

'This isn't nothing,' Spencer said, his tone teetering between anger and fear. 'Who did this to you? Did you do it to yourself?'

I reached out for his cock – that usually shuts him up. But unfortunately this time it didn't.

'I need an answer. Please. Something's going on. You're obviously being injured and I want to help you.'

I found myself welling up – partly because I was moved by how much he cared, but also because the surprise had been ruined.

*

The gym was a place of refuge to me: earphones in, Rihanna pumping messages of self-esteem into my head and no one from the college in sight. The gym was the last place any of them would be. They seemed to think that their bodies required no maintenance whatsoever because their souls were so squeaky clean. More than ever, the emphasis we place on body image can be destructive of course, but the positive impact of physical health on mental health is also well established. The college flock seemed so neglectful of their physical health and so bloody pious that I wondered if they were intentionally hastening their demise in order to get to the Pearly Gates quicker. Whatever their reasons, it meant the gym was my sanctuary from them. It didn't exactly slow down my dangerously accelerating weight loss, but it helped me work out my frustrations and filled me with the necessary endorphin rush which told me there was a light at the end of the very dark tunnel I'd been diverted through.

After one session, towelling off the sweat from my face which masked the tears dripping from my eyes, I noticed a flyer on the wall for pole fitness classes. I took down the number. It was something I'd always been curious about. You might know it as pole dancing, a term which conjures up images of strip clubs and half-naked ladies of the night rubbing themselves up and down a long phallic metal rod and wrapping their legs around it in impossible positions, while sex-starved men in the audience dream the pole is their own rigid little member.

Well, that's not what pole fitness is about – although, the idea that David or Madeline or the two snivelling cunts who grassed me up for complimenting them might think it is amused me no end. I could just see their faces if it got out that I was now a *pole dancer*. I have to admit this was one of the factors which spurred me on to book a taster session – that and the fact that it was a sport that involved great skill, agility and strength. Yes, a sport. There is an International Pole Dance Fitness Association, which holds the International Pole Championship every two years, and the session I was to attend was led by an IPC winner so I was quite nervous about going to the class.

Walking into the room was uncannily like walking into a church for the first time to lead a service – not that I sashayed down the aisle in hot pants and sports bra on that first service and hooked my legs over the pulpit hanging upside down while delivering my sermon, although I've come close. (We'll get to that later). But the pole room commanded a reverence of its own. It had its own unique and gleaming shrines, though they were poles rather than crosses. And it held great promise of lessons to be learned, skills to be acquired and strength to glean.

Fearing I would be late, which I felt would draw unwanted attention to me, I got there ridiculously early and had to hang around for half an hour outside the locked building. When a caretaker eventually opened it, I scurried inside and found the toilet. While I was having my anxiety induced wee, I heard two more women come in and from their excited chatter it was clear they were going to the taster session too. I flushed and hurried out attempting to attach myself to them – safety in numbers and all that.

'I read that a pair of fuck-me heels was essential,' I said showing off my new Pleasers.

The girls looked wide-eyed at me. It seemed that fuck-me heels were the last thing we would be needing.

Once we were in the dance studio I stood, back to the wall, feeling out of place and old. Yes, I was only in my mid-twenties, but as a mature student I was a veritable grandma compared to all the first-time undergrads in their late teens who had turned up to the class. Everyone except me seemed to know someone, so I was relieved when the only man in the class walked in alone. It must have taken some guts on his part to come here, so I took my strength from his.

'Hiya,' I said.

If I'm honest, I expected his voice to be as camp as Hadrian's, but his 'All right?' was deep and gruff, at odds with his nail polish.

'Come far?' I said as if I was on an awful first date.

'Just from Cherry Hinton. The wife dropped me off on her way to pick up our daughter from Guides.'

'You at the university?' I asked. We were on university property so I thought it was a decent enough question, but he turned his nose up as if I'd just let a pungent fart go.

'No, babe.'

'Oh, what do you do, then?'

'I work for the council. In the transport depot,' he said, slipping off his tracksuit to reveal some hot pants and a crop top. 'You?' he asked.

'I'm a priest,' I said. 'Or will be soon, I hope.'

The two girls I'd met in the toilet overheard and were hissing away at each other at my little revelation. The cross-dressing council mechanic didn't even flinch, of course – we became firm friends.

Finally our teacher arrived, looking eye-poppingly glamourous. Her name was Candy Apple – you couldn't make it up (though actually I just did, for confidentiality purposes, but her real name, trust me, is even more unbelievable) – and she certainly was sweet. She had a body to die for; one that made me feel horny and humiliated simultaneously. Her skin appeared to have been airbrushed by God, her boobs were made for resting your head on and her buttocks were indeed like fruit, which I found myself daydreaming about sinking my teeth into.

Candy told us we would start with a warm-up. Press-ups, sit-ups, that kind of thing. As I was a gym-goer my ability to do this kind of stuff was quite high compared to the other students, who, it became quickly apparent, were not regulars on a cross-trainer. So as they all grunted and groaned, I knocked out loads of reps like a boss and felt really smug about it.

When it came to actually getting on the pole to try the first move, I was suddenly brimming with confidence. Candy showed us a very simple spin.

'OK, go for it!' she nodded, as I volunteered to try.

I slipped down the pole like a drunk firefighter.

Yes, you need strength for this. Yes, you need agility – I mean, while hanging upside from a pole Candy Apple could spread her legs in ways that might have kept my coil consultant's ratings at one hundred percent if only I could have done the same that day in her surgery. But as Candy would show us like the exceptional teacher she was, what was most important was to understand the physics of what you were doing. Speed was essential. Launching yourself at the pole at the right velocity, angle and height was everything. But to do that took confidence. It took faith. Once again the parallels with the church weren't lost on me.

By the end of the lesson Candy had pushed me in all the right ways to find the courage to let go of my inhibitions and launch myself at the pole fast enough so that I could lift off and spin around the pole like a veteran. I went away feeling electric. I knew even then I wasn't a natural, that I probably wouldn't be competing at the IPC any time this century, but I found my achievements in class empowering. And to be in the presence of other women tapping into their mental and physical strength was inspiring.

The next day I couldn't move. I understood about delayed onset muscle soreness from the gym, but this was another level of ouch. And yet, I couldn't wait to get back next week. The bruises came thick and fast too. I fell off the pole so many times because I doubted my ability – and if that wasn't the perfect symbol for what I was going through in college (and would go through in the future) I don't know what is. With Candy's guidance the falls only served to spur me on, to help me grow in confidence and to have faith. Pole dancing was cathartic. It was healing – not just for me, but for many of the other women in the classes I went on to attend. The image of women always being scantily clad on a pole is correct, but it's not – in pole fitness at least – for the titillation of an audience of raincoated rotters. You need to have the side of your torso and arms free of clothes to help you grip the pole (and squeezing the pole hard enough to stay on was another source of bruises). Consequently, I often found myself in a studio with women of all shapes and sizes, all wearing not very much, all supporting each other, all free of judgement. Because it doesn't matter how big or small you are, what matters is: can you nail the move? And that takes thought, commitment and mental strength. We willed each other on, with a camaraderie which was the antithesis of the spirit of my college, and as a by-product our body confidence soared. Whenever someone nailed a move, beginner, intermediate or veteran, shrieks of delight, high fives and cries for someone to take a photo – QUICK! – filled the studio.

Like most addicts, I will always be in recovery when it comes to anorexia, but the pole fitness certainly helped me move through it. I am the most ungraceful person on a dance floor with moves like a crab cornered by a seafood chef, but that's OK because the greatest muscle required on the pole is found in the grey matter. If you think you can do it you'll smash it, but if you doubt yourself one *iota* (I knew those Greek lessons would come in handy at some point) you can hurt yourself.

I had kept the lessons a secret from Spencer. I planned to surprise him one day with an impromptu pole dance and dreamed of the smile on his face and the bulge in his pants when he saw me owning the pole. When he noticed the bruises in bed that morning, I was shocked at how emotional I was. I sobbed like a gold-digger with a prenup.

'I wanted it to be special. I was going to tell you but only when I was good enough to...'

He hugged me. 'Thank God.' He was so relieved that it was nothing more sinister, he couldn't stop smiling. Then he told me all about the Pink Pony in Atlanta, a very famous pole club, and offered next time he was there to go and do some research for me.

FOURTEEN

'Hello, dear.'

'Charlotte?' I sang it like a question because I couldn't quite believe she was standing at my door. I mean, of course it was her. There was no mistaking this beautiful boulder of a woman, but why would she have left the ivory tower of the principal's lodge and deigned to cross the court to my lowly quarters? I wanted to close the door on my untidy room and shimmy out into the corridor to hear what she had to say, but like the stone before the sepulchre, it seemed only supernatural forces could move her. So, 'Come in! Come in!' I said eventually, throwing discarded knickers under the bed and half-eaten sandwiches off of it.

'Don't worry about all that,' she said, filling the room with her spirit as much as her boobs. 'My rooms were much worse when I was a student.'

'What did you study?' I asked.

'English literature. Here at Cambridge.'

'Wow,' I said.

And we looked at each other in silence for what seemed like an hour before she said, 'I'm going to the cinema this evening. The Arts. They're playing a Fellini classic. Care to join me?'

Care to join me? Fascinating phrase. Full of soft unthreatening sounds, and yet if I didn't join her, did it imply that I didn't *care*? Anyway, I don't think I would have refused her invitation however she put it; I was too scared to. I was too beguiled by her to refuse.

So at 7 p.m. that evening I found myself nestled next to her maternal curves which overflowed from her seat into mine watching *La Dolce Vita* and wondering why I was there. Was Charlotte on a mission sent by David to keep an eye on me, correct me, or steer me on what he thought was the right course?

She must have read my mind, for she leant over and whispered, 'Does it feel like you're sleeping with the enemy?'

I was glad it was dark in the cinema; it covered my cheeks reddening. 'Well, perhaps fraternising with the person who sleeps with the enemy,' I said with a nervous giggle.

'Oh, David and I don't sleep together any more,' she said without a hint of embarrassment.

I nodded with just enough interest not to seem rude then pretended to be caught up in the adventures of Marcello Rubini and his fruitless search for love and happiness playing out on the screen before us.

*

'That was fun,' Charlotte beamed as we adjusted to the real world on the street a few hours later. 'Let's do it again soon.'

'Sure,' I said, a little unsure.

'In fact. There's this Lebanese restaurant I've been dying to try out. Shall we go on Saturday?'

'Saturday?' I said checking my mental diary. It wasn't jammed with appointments and Charlotte's gravitational force had not faded. So I said, 'OK.'

*

After stuffing ourselves with all manner of delectable dips, tabbouleh and mountains of pita that Saturday, Charlotte was already planning our next outing, which she said would be to the opera.

Since I'd had enough Dutch Courage, as we waited for the bill, I said, 'Does David not want to come and do these things with you?'

Charlotte took a deep breath, which nudged the entire table a few inches in my direction, and said, 'Let's just say, David and I don't share the same interests these days.'

She imbued the sentence with so many layers of meaning, that I knew in that moment that she wasn't just talking about their differing taste in cinema or food, but in the way he had dealt with me. I felt completely coddled in that moment and whenever we went out together after that. She wasn't sent by

David to keep me in line. Quite the opposite. She made sure we went out regularly, had a good time and laughed a lot. She was clearly taking me under her considerable bingo wing and not just because she wanted to protect me; I could tell she was also, rather naughtily, delighting in how her liaisons with me must have pissed David off no end. And for the same reason, I couldn't help delighting in them too.

Spoiler alert! I get married in a few chapters' time. By then, Charlotte and I had been getting along so famously, and infamously, that she even offered to make my wedding cake. However, if she made my cake, then of course she would be invited to the wedding and the possibility that David would accompany her, no matter how slim, was just too stomach churning for me, so that was the first time I ever refused Charlotte anything.

FIFTEEN

It was election time. A time of such sedative power as to be rivalled only by rectal diazepam. A time that was like Christmas these days – it went on far too long and saw old white men in ridiculous suits parading around telling us what they'd give us if we did the right thing. I'm talking about general elections, of course. But at the college, like all universities up and down the country, there were annual elections too; for the president of the Junior Common Room, the JCR – our name for the college's student union. Yes, Cambridge always had to be different from every other university. I mean, Magdalene College has to be pronounced *Maudleyn*. What's that all about? Something to do with Lord Audley, the founder, who liked the resonance the 15th Century English pronunciation of Magdalene had with his own name, the vain little twat. You'd think we in the theological college might have something to say about the desecration of Mary Magdalene's name, but no, that's just the way it has always been so we don't question it. And maintaining the status quo was what it was all about when it came to our little elections too.

'There's only one person standing for president,' Tony said when he found me and Hadrian playing a game of *Snog, Shag, Marry* to the photos of the faculty on the wall of the common room.

'So?' Hadrian said, still musing over whether to shag or marry Dr Lebonza – it was a tough call; he was quite the beefcake.

'So,' Tony explained, 'we don't live in a dictatorship. There should be a choice.'

'Who's standing?' I asked, more impatient to hear Hadrian's decision on Dr Lebonza than Tony's answer.

'Karen,' he snarled.

'Karen?' I hissed.

Karen was a Karen long before being a Karen became a thing. In fact it wouldn't surprise me if college Karen was the inspiration for the whole Karen meme. She was one of the mirthless women that decided to tell tales to teacher that I complimented her (usually poorly presented) rack. It appears the second years, of which she was one, had decided that only they should be eligible to stand for election. The 'unruly' first years, of which I was one, were deemed inappropriate leaders – presumably because we were either gay, black, young, unmarried or knew how to dress – and so the election hadn't even been discussed with us.

'We can't let her stand alone,' I said, suddenly interested in politics.

Hadrian piped up, 'Well, I'd hate for the passion to go out of our relationship, but I'd have to marry him, just so I could shag him more than once. I mean, there's so much I'd like to do to him. Once wouldn't be enough.'

'Eh?' I said.

'Dr Lebonza,' he replied.

'Forget Dr Lebonza!' I said. 'This is serious.'

'It is,' Tony said. 'So I'm going to stand as well.'

'Me too,' Gary piped up from the corner of the room where he was reading a newspaper.

The three of us turned to look at our fellow first year.

'Don't worry,' he said to Tony, 'not against you, mate. I'm going to stand for treasurer.'

'Excellent idea,' I said.

I couldn't wait for the hustings, not just to see the look on Karen's face when Tony, a fully paid-up member up of the Labour party, got up to speak, but also when Gary took to the lectern and announced:

'As an ex-drug dealer who has done time for embezzlement and fraud, I am the perfect person for the job of treasurer of the JCR.'

I was delighted as the jaws of the assembled second years dropped as one.

'Seriously,' Gary said with only a dash of sarcasm, 'I am very good with money. I did a roaring trade in crystal meth till I lost focus through the alcoholism and got myself nicked.'

The few first years in the room applauded like an arena full of rock fans as Gary grinned like the star he was.

I had a lot of time for Gary. Not because he had a chequered past, but because reform, transformation and forgiveness are at the very heart of our church and I can't think of anyone who embodies reform and transformation quite like Gary. I admire anyone who can not only overcome their addictions but do such a phenomenal handbrake turn on their lives and screech off in such a new and positive direction. That's why, at our next communion, I was concerned to see Gary stand so abruptly after taking the communion bread and wine and stride from the chapel, his eyes glistening as if he was grieving.

I knew something was seriously wrong, and after taking communion myself I had a pretty good idea of what it was, so I left the service too and went up to his room.

'Are you OK, Gaz?' I said quietly, knocking lightly on the door, which was ajar.

I could see he was bent over the washbasin as if he'd been sick, toothbrush gripped in his fist. He shook his head in response to my question and spat some mouthwash into the bowl.

'Need to talk?' I said as he dried his mouth and sat on the end of his bed, head in hands.

'I've been in recovery for twelve years,' he sighed.

'That's amazing,' I said, edging into the room.

'Did you taste the wine?' he asked.

'Yep,' I said sitting next to him.

'There was alcohol in it.'

I'd tasted it too, but I said pathetically, 'Are you sure? Maybe it was just off. You know our church forbids alcohol in—'

''Course I'm bloody sure,' he snapped before putting an apologetic hand on my arm. 'But I was only sure when my mouth was full of it. That's why I had to get out of there so I could spit it out,' he said gesturing to a patch of grass outside where the wine no doubt still soaked the blades like the scene of a crime.

And indeed it was a crime. What Gary told me next has stayed with me ever since and had a huge impact on the way I run my churches.

'Alcoholics are always in recovery,' he explained. 'Every single day you wake up it's like the first day of being sober all over again and you pray to God that you have the strength to get through that one day. Alcohol destroyed my life and my relationships with those I love. So I came to the Lord's table to find support and redemption and nothing has helped me more to make a change than God. And just now when I took a drink from the cup of salvation I found something that I thought I would never ever find there. As soon as that stuff touched my tongue, all the demons of my addiction surged through me again, after all this time. But I had not relapsed. This was not my doing. I did not consent to drink that booze. I never dreamed I would have to worry about those demons here in this church, in my place of sanctuary. I can't tell you how shocking and painful that was.'

'Who the fuck would be so dumb as to order the wrong wine?' I seethed, praying that this wasn't some sick attempt to oust the pretender to the treasurer's throne.

*

When it came to voting day, I and all the other disgruntled first years happily put our pencil cross next to Tony's and Gary's names and I asked God to help me find the strength not to draw two huge saggy melons next to Karen's. But just when we thought voting was over, Karen's husband (also a student at the college) strode into the common room and shoved a fistful of extra voting forms into the ballot box.

'Er... Excuse me!' Tony said, who'd have had international observers standing by if he could. 'What are those?'

'Those?' Karen's spouse said reddening ever so slightly. 'Those are postal votes. Just came in.' He turned and attempted to stride out again.

'Woah, woah, woah!' I said, stopping him in his tracks. 'Where the hell are these postal votes coming from?' I clawed at the space between us as I drew the most aggressive air quotes ever round the words *postal votes*. 'I didn't know this college had students spread all over the globe. Where are they? Helping Dr Price's poor black children in Africa?'

Karen's husband had no response. Of course.

'Ooh,' I said, picking up some forms and hacking away at them with a pencil. 'These votes were phoned in earlier. I forgot to add them.' I stuffed my fake votes into the ballot box and the common room erupted into such a melee that the principal himself quickly appeared.

'That's it!' he declared. 'I am suspending the constitution.' And after a conflab with his fellow tutors outside which was miraculously brief following such an extreme and drastic action, politically speaking, he came back in and simply declared Karen the winner with all the democratic integrity of Donald Trump.

Yes, this whole episode is just a load of badly dressed snooty twats playing at being grown-ups – it's hardly actual national politics, which is, of course, by contrast... um... a load of badly dressed snooty twats playing at being grown-ups – but this breakdown of relations in a theological college could have been the perfect moment for our teachers to demonstrate how ministers can serve as negotiators of peace and reconciliation between parties in conflict. Instead, they kept their well established and barnacled boat from being rocked by throwing any alternative voices overboard.

If being a Christian means anything in the twenty-first century it must be that we celebrate diversity. If we believe God made us, then he made us as we are – all different. He intended us to be this way and it is not for the white middle-aged men who dominate to force us round- or crescent- or star-shaped pegs into their square holes.

Things were broken in the college. It was like a re-enactment of the eminent Stanford psychologist Philip Zimbardo's famous Prison Study, during which, after randomly assigning twenty-four ordinary, psychologically healthy college students to roles of prisoners and guards, giving each group suitably depersonalizing attire (the guards wore reflective sunglasses, for example), the students began very quickly to lose their everyday personalities and fulfil their assigned roles. Guards quickly began giving prisoners humiliating menial tasks, then forced them to strip naked and subjected them to sexual degradation. Within thirty-six hours, the first healthy student prisoner had a breakdown and the experiment was abandoned after just six days, because it was out of control.

Now, I'm not saying I or any of my fellow students were stripped naked and subjected to sexual degradation – unless you include Piers's pathetic attempts to finger me in the bar as sexual degradation, in which case I *am* saying we were subject to sexual degradation. I'm definitely not saying Karen and her Trumpish husband wore reflective sunglasses – that would be way too cool for them. But what Zimbardo used his experiments to argue is that there are no bad apples, only bad barrels.

Zimbardo served as an expert witness for the defence of one of the guards who'd been tried for the atrocities at Abu Ghraib prison, where US army reservists tortured and humiliated Iraqi prisoners. Despite the natural repulsion it is easy to feel toward those guards, Zimbardo's aim was to show how readily, given the right circumstances, almost any normal person can become an agent of evil.

I'm not drawing a parallel between Abu Ghraib and my little college on the banks of the river Cam – although Madeline White would no doubt fit in perfectly there – but there is a link and it's not far-fetched. Most anti-religious people will see religion as the cause of all wars (conveniently forgetting about oil, as they drive their diesel cars home to their fossil fuelled homes), but if the churches, mosques, temples of the world are training their future messengers in such environments as found in my college with its my-way-or-the-highway attitude, then I can understand why religion might well be seen as a canker that catalyses conflict.

Zimbardo called his findings the Lucifer Effect. And I spent my remaining college years living with Spencer and commuting all the way in to classes every day in an attempt to minimise the effect of the rotten barrel on me. It also minimised my chances of being found crawling along the court pissed in the early hours, turning up to services and canapé parties with a few million creamy hitchhikers, or building another Wall of Shame on my windowsill.

SIXTEEN

It was on my commute one day that I saw Madeline approaching the college in her car – the sled must have been in for an MOT. She stopped down the street and let out her passenger, Ruth.

Ruth was a student at the college. She was considerably older than me and had heeded God's call to become a minister later in life. She was one of many middle-aged people who apparently hear God calling to them all their life and at a certain point in time they cannot ignore it any longer. This moment usually coincides rather conveniently with the moment they are made redundant and are finding it too hard to find another job at their age.

Ruth used to be a highflyer in the City. She was articulate, clever, well-educated. I liked her. She was also married to a sweet guy called Rob, until a few months ago. Perhaps he wasn't so sweet after all. Who knows? That was their business.

She jumped out of Madeline's car and placed a smacker right on the White Witch's lips, before walking the last few metres into college as Madeline drove in. Now it was my business.

'If you're going to do a sneaky drop-off, this is too close, ladies,' I thought. They clearly weren't experts in the etiquette of extra-marital affairs. But what concerned me more was that Madeline White, the erstwhile custodian of my pastoral care, head tutor in the college, was flagrantly flouting the first rule of college: don't fuck the students. I was transported back to those crotch-clenchingly awkward moments when Madeline told me I had been inappropriate in my behaviour and sentenced me to a stint on a Shut The Fuck Up course and an extra year in this shithole as if she was the governess of Wentworth. Inappropriate? Ina-fucking-ppropriate? I'll give you inappropriate. It doesn't matter that Ruth was *old enough to know better*, as my dear old mum used to say; Madeline was in a position of authority and power, and in case her moral compass was having problems finding magnetic north there was always the college policy to fall back on which clearly forbad such relations.

Madeline was thankfully not my personal tutor by this time. I was now looked after with considerably more sensitivity by a tutor called Rachel. When I say considerably more sensitivity, she would ask me once in a while if I was eating enough, I would say yes and that was that. But that was some improvement, as indeed it would have been if I'd had Chairman Mao in charge of my pastoral care.

Rachel and I were having an end of term meeting shortly after I first saw Madeluth, Radeline, whatever their mash-up name might be. I had seen them together in various places around college since, where they would try to look like they weren't anything more than acquaintances, but Madeline's annoying little cockapoo would always head straight for Ruth and sniff about between her legs, revelling in the familiarity of that particular odour which was no doubt smeared all over Madeline's residence. I could have said nothing, but would that have made me as culpable as Madeline in all this? Almost.

'Rachel... um... I want to share... well, I don't want to, but I feel like I have to tell you something.'

'Of course,' Rachel smiled reassuringly. 'Fire away!'

'Um... Well, you see...' Wow! I sounded like Madeline herself trying to spit out my terribly *inappropriate* misdemeanours. 'OK...' I took a deep breath. 'I think that Madeline White and Ruth Fraser are having a relationship.'

Rachel's response was not what I expected. She put her head in her hands for a moment, then when she had gathered herself, she straightened up and said, 'It's worse than that.'

'Oh?'

'They *are* having an affair,' Rachel confirmed, 'but Madeline has been to David and told him all about it. He drew up a contract signed by Madeline, Ruth and the college which outlines how they must conduct themselves, you know, what they can be seen to be doing and what they can't, so they can continue with the relationship.'

'So David condones this?' I said, agape.

Rachel shrugged. 'Well, he certainly hasn't stopped it.'

'But it's a safeguarding issue,' I said.

'Not any more, according to the college.'

I wondered if Philip Zimbardo would like to come and conduct his next experiment here in my vicar school.

SEVENTEEN

The interminable Narnian winter of my college years eventually turned to spring. I graduated at last and hurried off to my first appointment as a fully-fledged priest, putting on my dog collar for the first time like a bride-to-be donning a tiara in the bridal shop, something which I did do shortly after, when I was trying on dresses for my own wedding to Spencer – just for a laugh. I wasn't really going to wear a bloody tiara to my wedding; I was a bride, not a toddler watching *Frozen*.

To wear a dog collar while training was expressly forbidden, which I thought was a bad idea. You at least needed to give it a test drive in public. You need to get used to people staring at you in the street and in the shop. You need to grow accustomed to the fact that people will look in your basket in Sainsbury's and see the bottle of wine with the Tampax and raise their eyebrows – I'm not sure which worries them more, the booze or the fact that I have a functioning womb. So, never one to take the word of my tutors with anything but a quarry of salt, I decided to wear it when I went into town one day with my brother George, who was still very much local since his six-week emigration.

We mooched. I love a bit of mooching. We mooched in the vinyl shops. We mooched in the clothing stores. And it was as I was holding a skirt up for George's opinion that he nudged me.

'Everyone's staring at you,' he said.

'Are you sure it's not you?' I said, deadpan.

'Why would they be staring at me?'

'Well, those jeans are awfully tight.'

'Fuck off!' he said before checking his arse out in the mirror. 'It's the dog collar.'

Of course it was. I looked in the mirror too. I had this paranoid feeling everyone was staring because they knew I was a fraud, not a real priest just yet. But it was no such thing. They had no idea who I was, they just saw the dog collar and they stared. Like they still do to this day. The funny thing is, the stares don't just come from lay people. We clergy folk stare at each other's clerical shirts and collars too, like schoolkids in the playground checking out who has the coolest take on the uniform. There's a whole rainbow of colours to choose from when it comes to shirts and even a range of styles. The Dr Prices of the world will come back from West Africa sporting highly decorated shirts made of local fabric in the buba style. It would look great on a local, but when the pasty white priest wears it in Bognor Regis he looks like a dog in a Santa Claus costume. Some priests go for the blue or grey shirt in an attempt to eschew the traditional black, but to me they look like they're about to get their school photo taken. So when it comes to the clerical shirt, I am perhaps more traditional than in any other part of my life. I go for the black. So does Hadrian, but he says it's because it's slimming. I think I'm just so proud to be a priest that I want there to be no doubt about what I am to the public. Yes, I'm a proper priesty priest. But not so as a bride. I had bought my blood-red wedding dress for eighty quid on eBay from China and the white cloak and train, which some might say looked as if it was made from a net curtain, was made from a net curtain – and was fabulous.

After we were married, Spencer and this proper priesty priest moved into their very own manse in their very own parish. It was palatial compared to the glorified cell I'd been living in for the past three years and had enough rooms for me to install a pole in one – my very own pole fitness room.

As I settled into the manse on my first official morning at work, the phone rang.

'Hello?' I said trying somehow to inject everything I hoped to be into that one word: approachable, supportive, knowledgeable, in control.

'Well, hello,' came a voice so slimy down the other end of the line that I could almost see him twisting the ends of a hipster moustache. 'You must be the new priest. I've been so looking forward to meeting you.'

'Oh?'

'I'm Julian, Julian Sloane, the funeral director, and I've got a funeral for you to do.'

Shit! Already? Couldn't everyone just wait a bit before they start popping off? At least until I get settled. What was I supposed to do? How do I *do* a funeral? I'd been at college for one year more than most priests and yet I still had no fucking clue. If someone had called up and asked me to quote Leviticus, no problem; if they'd asked me to conjugate a Greek verb, I might have stood a chance; if I'd been asked to bake unleavened bread fit for the Last Supper then I could even stretch to that, but to do a funeral... I had no idea, mainly because neither did our tutors, who'd been tutors for so many years they'd completely lost touch with doing anything practical and useful that a priest does.

'Um... OK,' I squeaked down the phone sounding neither approachable, supportive, knowledgeable, nor in control. 'When would this be?'

'Next week. Thursday.'

'Next week?' I yelped.

'Well, I'd love to give you more notice, but we usually have to wait until the deceased has actually died and wrap things up before they rot, so we have a relatively small window for these things.'

'Yes, yes, of course,' I tittered. *Smart arse*, I thought. 'No problem. Leave it with me.'

As soon as I'd hung up on Julian, the phone rang again.

'Hello?' I said trying to hide the dread in my voice.

'Can I speak to the vicar?' said the voice of a harpy with strep.

'I'm the priest,' I corrected the old girl gently.

'Yeah, well, can I speak to the vicar?' she said impatiently.

'I am the vicar,' I said through gritted teeth, 'but we're called priests here.'

'What, coz you're a woman?'

'No. That's just what we're called. Women and men.'

'Christ, I can't keep up with all this political correctness these days. So we can't have a man?'

'To do what?'

'To marry us.'

'You want to book a wedding?'

'Yeah.'

'Oh, right.' Bloody hell, I hoped all days would not be as busy as this one. 'And who is it getting married?' I had almost as little knowledge of what to do when someone calls up for a wedding as I did about a funeral, except the fact that I'd been married myself just weeks before meant some of the procedure was still fresh in my mind.

'Me and my Ricky.'

'You?' I blurted out, before chastising myself for judging. Actually, how nice, I thought, to marry an old couple who've found love again.

When I turned up at Ricky's mum's house where he was living with Candice, his wife to be, his eight younger siblings and ten dogs, I was shocked to see both Ricky and Candice were not likely to be getting their bus passes any time soon. Candice had some incredible bingo wings that were as tattooed as the rest of the skin that her vest top rendered visible, and Ricky was struggling to cling onto the few nicotine-stained teeth left in his mouth, but they were both in their twenties. The fact that they smoked liked power plants perhaps explained why Candice sounded older than her years on the phone.

'Cup of tea?' Candice said as we settled in the living room.

'Yes please,' I said politely. You become an expert in stomaching all sorts of tea when you're a priest – from builder's tea you can stand your spoon up in, to herbal ones that smell like your nan's potpourri.

Candice sighed – well, it must have been a great effort to get up off the red PVC sofa. She went out to the kitchen. 'Ange, do the vicar a tea, will you?' I heard her say to Ricky's mum.

'Vicar? More like a tart in that dress,' I heard Ange mutter.

It was a warm late summer's day, so I was wearing a black skirt which stopped above the knee and nude-coloured tights. This is why I go for the traditional black shirt with the dog collar – the rest of my outfit often challenges some people so much I'm not sure they could handle anything too jazzy on top. Of course, if a male priest had turned up wearing shorts – or even a mankini, for that matter – I'm sure Ange would have said how summery he looked and complimented him on the practicality of what he was wearing in this heat.

I had come to do the wedding prep. Nothing to do with dresses, bridesmaids, bouquets, seating plans or cake design – no, I always left all those personal details to the people it means the most to: the bride's and bridegroom's mothers. I was there to help Bridezilla and her spouse-to-be take the foot off the gas of the marital juggernaut for a moment and take time to consider the spiritual. Think about the big questions, like 'What does marriage mean to you? Have you talked about the financial implications? Have you talked about children? If you don't want children, but you become pregnant what will you do? If you want children and you find out you're carrying a baby with Down's syndrome, will that change anything and, if so, why?' I didn't say all this in my opening gambit; that would be cruel. I spaced this out over a few visits over two weeks. Today, I started with, 'How do you think marriage will change your relationship?'

This is the part where I hope they don't say, 'It won't, we'll always love each other just as much as we do now.'

Because then I'd be compelled to ask, 'If it won't change a thing then why are you getting married?'

But Candice and Ricky were no fools, they knew exactly why they were getting married.

'It's great for tax, innit?' Candice said. 'It's like we save seventy quid each a year.'

'Yeah, and I'm getting the complete Blu-ray box set of *Breaking Bad* with my seventy quid.' Ricky grinned so widely I was worried his one remaining incisor would be squeezed out.

I sneaked a peek skywards. 'Hiya, Lord, I think we need to talk.'

EIGHTEEN

Next Thursday was hurtling towards me like a cartoon anvil so I hightailed it round to Linda, the widow of the deceased, to talk about the funeral. But before that I called Hadrian.

'What the fuck am I supposed to ask her?' I said down the phone.

'Well, you need to gather some stories for the eulogy.'

'Obvs.'

'And then remember what they said in college.'

'Which bit?'

'People will want to talk about the meaning of life and why do we die. They will want to discuss the resurrection and have questions about the afterlife.'

Hadrian was right of course. There wasn't a bigger question than death. If there was ever a purpose that religion served, which we could agree on the world over, it was to try and make sense of death. Be prepared, they told us, it will be as emotionally exhausting for you as it will be for the grieving, so empty your diary after any funeral or funeral visit because you will need time to recover.

I sat down on one of Linda's chintzy wing-backed chairs and surreptitiously looked at the list of big questions Hadrian had helped me compile as she brought in tea so sweet Willy Wonka would be proud.

'So how are you?' I said gently. 'You must have a lot of questions at this time.'

'I do,' she said, sighing orgasmically as she settled in her chair, a preserve of the aged, as much as farting without acknowledging it and having full blown conversations loudly with yourself, all of which Linda managed to do in the short time I was with her. 'The main question I have is: can we have Sinatra singing "My Way" at the end?'

I was thrown off course a little by this particular question – it didn't quite have the philosophical angle I was ready for.

'That's no problem,' I said. 'And... um... what about you? How do you feel about—?'

'Hymns?' Linda said. 'I couldn't give a toss really, but Liam liked "The Lord is my Shepherd", so can we have that?'

I smiled through gritted teeth – not just because she didn't care about the hymns but because the one she'd chosen was about as original at a funeral as having 'Come on Eileen' at a wedding reception. I nodded anyway.

Linda went on to make sure I knew that Liam supported Spurs, that he loved his grandkids and had been a regular at the Moon and Stars pub for forty years. If I remembered to talk about such salient points and didn't forget to play 'My Way' at the end, then, 'That's all sorted.' She brushed her hands together as if she had just finished baking a cake, and it was evident that she was done.

As Hadrian had reminded me, I had cleared my diary after this meeting in order to have the time to recuperate. From what? But the time wasn't wasted. I called up my steward, Erin. It was her job to set up the church for services – opening up, making sure the lights are on, the chairs are in the right place, the sound system is working, handing out the order of service. She was a real asset.

'Hi, Erin. It looks like we have a funeral next Thursday.'

'I'll be right round,' she said.

I began to tell her that that wasn't necessary; that I could tell her everything I needed her to do over the phone, but she had already hung up and within a few creepily short minutes there was a knock on my door.

'Hi,' Erin said somewhat out of breath. 'I came as fast as I could.'

'Well, you shouldn't have worried,' I smiled. 'We could have—'

'Well, we haven't properly met yet, so I thought it would be a good chance to...' she said looking over my shoulder.

'Come in!' I smiled, since that was clearly what she was dying to do.

'Glass of wine?' I said.

She looked at me a little baffled; it was still early.

So I explained, 'I've just been to visit the widow about the funeral next week. Things can get very emotional. It takes it out of you.'

'Oh, I see,' Erin smiled. 'In that case, I'd love one.'

I invited Erin to sit as I poured the wine, but instead she mooched around the kitchen like my brother in a vinyl shop.

'I like what you've done with the place,' she said, poking her head through to the living room. 'Much less stuffy than when Brian was here. Nice to have someone young for a change.'

Erin wasn't a great deal older than me. It would be nice for me to have her around too, I thought, as she disappeared upstairs.

'Mind if I do the tour?' she said, not waiting for permission.

I followed her upstairs, hoping I'd remembered to put my rampant rabbit away.

'Oh!' I heard her say as she came to the landing.

Perhaps I hadn't.

'Are you having problems with the ceiling?' she said as I caught her up.

'Sorry?'

'The scaffolding,' she said, peering into the pole room.

A little laugh of relief escaped me. 'No, no. It's meant to be there. It's a pole. For pole fitness.'

Erin looked a little blank.

'Pole dancing,' I said.

And Erin's eyes popped out on cartoon stalks. She looked at the pole, then at me. And then at the pole. And then at me again.

'You... do...'

'It's a very good way to keep fit,' I explained before she jumped to any sordid conclusion. 'Want a go?'

After attacking the pole with all the gusto and lack of success of me on my first lesson, Erin decided drinking wine in the living room was more her sport and, after a glass or two, she was telling me all about the lack of sex in her life and how she worried about the amount of time she found herself masturbating. I thought it was time to show her the rampant rabbit after all and reassure her that masturbation was no bad thing.

'I've never told anyone about that,' she said with a giggle of relief. 'It wasn't the kind of thing I could talk to Brian about.'

I poured her some more wine.

'Now what about this funeral?' she said. 'They haven't asked for "Bat out of Hell" again, have they?'

NINETEEN

It was time for my first staff meeting. This was to be attended by all the dog collar wearers in the area and chaired by Peter, who I would soon come to call Uncle Peter, since he was the kind of cuddly avuncular soul you dream about having as a supervisor. There were just three of us under Peter's downy wing, and after we'd all settled around the meeting room table – with tea and cake, of course – Peter began.

'So. On the agenda today we have annual leave requests, orders to the publishing house, the upcoming synod, but since we have a new member of our team here today, let's start by officially introducing ourselves, shall we? How about we go around and just say your name and a little about yourself.'

I recalled Dr Price saying something similar back in college and me perverting the meaning of a Psalm to raise a laugh. However, though I'd only known Uncle Peter for about four minutes, already I couldn't bear the thought of being the object of his disappointment, so I told myself to tone it down this time.

'Hi,' said the priest to Peter's left with a warm smile in my direction, a Vicar of Dibley type, but with a grey bob instead of black, and, surprisingly, it seemed, if their moniker was anything to go by, a penis. 'I'm Keith. I live at the manse in Havelow with my partner and our three gorgeous cats and... Well, that's all I can really think of to say,' he said, flapping his hands in his face as he reddened.

'I'm Patricia,' said the next priest gruffly as if she wanted to show Keith how a real man spoke. 'I arrived here last year. Before that I was in the Cotswolds, which actually was my first appointment.'

I raised my eyebrows in gentle curiosity as Patricia was clearly close to retirement age.

'Yes, I came to the church late. Although I heard God calling me for a long while I resisted his call, for twenty years in fact, until I could resist it no longer.'

Which, it turned out, just like Ruth of Madeluth fame, coincided nicely with the time Patricia was made redundant from Marks and Sparks. She talked about ignoring God's call as if it were a heroic endeavour. Personally, I'd question the integrity of my faith if I heard God calling me for two decades and all that time said 'No, God, fuck off, I've got better things to do'. But I chose not to share that in my first staff meeting.

Instead, as it was now my turn, I chirped, 'Hello, everyone. So nice to be here. I'm so excited to start working alongside you all in this, my very first appointment. I live in the manse in Littleford with my husband Spencer. He's a pilot...'

Keith let out a little oral fart of excitement, then put his fingers over his mouth by way of an apology, encouraging me to continue.

'Actually,' I went on, 'I was so nervous about being late today that I arrived half an hour early. And since Spencer's been away on some long-haul flights for the past week and I've been feeling ridiculously horny without him around to sort me out, I popped in the toilet there and had a good wank before you lot arrived. It was such a relief, I can tell you. Now I'm ready and focused. So, what's the order of business for today?'

OK, I didn't exactly *say* that last bit, but thirty minutes earlier, as I hitched up my knickers and breathed a sigh of orgasmic relief, I thought, 'I must tell Erin about this when I see her.'

With introductions out of the way and no faux pas from me, Peter went on to explain how there were thirty churches in the area, which would be divided up among the four of us. Peter, Keith and Patricia would have a whopping eight each to look after, which left a mere six for me. Peter was going easy on me as the newbie, but even so that meant on Sundays, even with a local preacher to take some services, I would have to do a 9 a.m., 11 a.m., 2 p.m. and 6:30 p.m. service. That would often leave me little time to get across to the next parish and I'd be chomping at the bit to leave after a service while nodding politely as older members of the congregation over-shared the details of their latest urinary tract infection with me and busybodies tried to rope me into their curtain twitching schemes disguised as caring for the community.

'Fuck me,' I muttered. 'If I wanted to do a 9-5 I would have been a secretary.'

'Sorry,' Peter smiled. 'Did you want to say something?'

'Oh…' I stuttered. 'Just thinking how lovely these cakes are. Where are they from?'

'Ah,' Peter said, gesturing theatrically to his left, 'that's Keith's department.'

'They're from Pret,' Keith said proudly. 'On the High Street. They do a lovely cream horn too,' he added with a wink and I wondered if he had arrived at the meeting earlier than I had thought.

TWENTY

Linda was in the majority when it came to not being inclined to explore with me the deeper meaning of what grief presented to those left behind. And she was joined in that majority by the family of Dave.

Dave had died relatively young at sixty – probably from cirrhosis of the liver if his drinking habits were anything like the rest of his family. They were chugging Special Brew at ten in the morning when I went to do the funeral visit, all of them: Dave's three brothers, their wives, his mum and her grandkids, who looked barely old enough to drink legally. But then, who was I to judge them on how much they drank? They had just lost a beloved son, brother and uncle – I'd be necking more than a few glasses of gin if I were them.

They lived on the same estate as Candice and Ricky and I mentioned their imminent wedding by way of small talk as the obligatory cuppa was made – they didn't offer me any booze.

'Well, they ain't invited to the funeral, bunch of cunts,' said Dave's brother, Jim.

'Oi, you,' his mum Sonia screeched – which I soon learnt wasn't a screech at all, it was her normal speaking voice. When she eventually did screech all the glasses in the display cabinet nearly shattered. 'Don't swear in front of the priest, for God's sake.'

'It's fine,' I said. 'Actually I swear like a trooper myself, but I never blaspheme,' I said, gently and indirectly chastising her for her oath.

'You what?' Sonia snapped – which I soon learnt wasn't a snap at all, it was her default way of replying to anything.

'You took the Lord's name in vain,' Jim said, enjoying getting one up on his mum.

'Blimey,' Sonia mumbled sulkily into her lager. 'Sorr-ee.'

'So...' I began, but after my experience with Linda I decided to hold off on the bigger questions and start with,

'...music. What kind of music would you like at the funeral?'

'"My Way",' Sonia said.

'Fuck off!' another of Dave's brothers, Kurt, piped up. And I was inclined to agree with him. 'We're having "Ring of Fire" by Johnny Cash at the end.' He grinned ghoulishly.

'Don't be so bleeding stupid!' Sonia said.

'That's what he wanted. We've got to follow his wishes, ain't we, vicar?' Jim chimed in.

I'm not a fucking vicar. 'Well,' I offered, 'we will be in a crematorium, won't we?'

'So?' said Kurt.

'It might not be very appropriate,' I said, waiting for the penny to drop.

'But that's the point!' Kurt cackled. 'It's bloody funny, innit?'

Jim cackled too.

'We'll have "My Way" at the start then,' Sonia said.

I looked around at Dave's young nieces and nephews. One of them – thankfully not drinking – was barely a teenager. She was huddled in the corner of the sofa next to her scowling brother, his arm protectively around her. I thought all this arguing about song choice might not be what the little ones needed to here, so I decided to move on.

'So tell me all about Dave!' I said, pen poised to make some notes for the eulogy.

It wasn't a case of you could cut the air with a knife, more you could possibly make a nick in it with an industrial strength chainsaw. The niece squirmed her way off the sofa and tearfully hurried out pursued by her brother.

'It's a difficult time, I know,' I said softly. 'But this is a moment when we can look back fondly at Dave and all the exciting things he got up to. The things he did for fun, for example.'

Jim and Kurt looked at each other as if I'd just taken their lager away. So Kurt's wife, Andrea, stepped up.

'He liked football,' she said.

'Great,' I said with as much enthusiasm as I could muster about grown men getting paid more than a small African country's national debt on a weekly basis to kick a ball about while supporters fulfilled their primaeval desire to make war in the absence of a real threat. 'And who did he support?'

'He was a Gunner.'

'Arsenal, eh?' I said, writing this down. 'Hope he doesn't bump into Liam up there.'

'Who?' Kurt said.

'Oh, nothing,' I smiled. 'And what else did he get up to?'

I watched Sonia, Kurt and Jim play ping pong with each other's eyes.

'He liked running the youth club, didn't he?' Andrea added. 'He did it voluntarily.'

'Oh wow. This is great. He was generous with his time. Helping the youth,' I noted.

'You don't need to mention that,' Sonia waved away Andrea's contribution.

'Did Dave have a wife or kids?' I asked.

Sonia shook her head.

'What did he do for a living?'

'On the dole,' Jim said.

'Hobbies?'

Everyone shrugged. I could see this was going nowhere. But that was OK. Here I was, a stranger coming into their lives at this terrible time and asking them for the life story of the person they've lost. Perhaps talking about him was making the sense of loss more acute. Perhaps it was simply difficult to remember. I could barely remember what I came upstairs for sometimes.

'Well, if you think of any more things you want me to say, just give me a call. And if I can help in any other way, if anyone just wants to talk, then I'm here.'

I finished my tea, wishing it had a drop of Special Brew in it, and left the family to get on with grieving.

TWENTY-ONE

The following week I stood sombrely with Julian the funeral director outside the crematorium as the hearse arrived.

Julian loved his job. I think it was the costume that did it for him most of all. The top hat, tails and cane. I think he thought he was the Lord Flashheart of undertakers; an irresistible sex symbol to every woman he came across, including me. The first time we met in person, he burst through the doors of the church and stood framed in the archway bellowing, 'Ah, you must be the new priest. Keith *said* you were gorgeous.' Erin and I were setting up for a Sunday service at the time. She swooned and nipped off to the toilet to sort herself out. I sighed.

Today, we both bowed to the coffin as Dave's family tumbled out of the cars behind, all clutching beers. The only time I didn't see them with a tinnie in their hands was during the funeral itself, otherwise I might have believed they'd had the cans surgically fixed to their palms.

'Ready?' Julian said to me.

'Everyone ready?' I said gently to the family.

'Yep,' Jim said.

'No,' Sonia said. 'I'm dying for a wee.'

That'll be the barrel of lager you've had this morning, I thought, as I directed her to the ladies.

When all the faffing was done and the congregation inside, it was time to draw the coffin from the hearse. Did I say all the faffing was done? Jim and Kurt had insisted they get 'stuck in' and help the professional pallbearers Julian had brought along. I cringed at the inevitable car crash that would ensue.

'Thank you, gentlemen,' Julian said, his signal for the bearers to begin pulling out the coffin from the car.

Jim and Kurt elbowed their way in and grabbed a handle.

'Thank you, gentlemen,' he said again, the sign for them to raise it onto their shoulders.

Jim and Kurt reddened and shuddered like Olympic weightlifters.

'Fuck me. He's heavy,' Kurt growled.

'You're holding it in the wrong place,' Jim snapped.

'Expert in carrying coffins, are you, now?' Kurt hissed. 'Move forward! You're in my way.'

'Sir,' Julian said tactfully to Kurt, 'it would be really helpful if you came around this side.' And thus he separated the brothers like schoolboys who distracted each other in class.

Once the Laurel and Hardy show was over, Julian and I processed towards the crem in front of the coffin.

'So how did you find the family?' Julian said out of the corner of his mouth.

'Well, they weren't the most talkative, so this isn't going to be the longest eulogy you've ever had to sit through.'

Julian snorted, 'I bet they weren't.'

'What do you mean?' I frowned.

'How did you feel when they told you?'

'Told me what?'

'The news.'

'What news?'

Julian looked at me mischievously. His face was smug with knowing.

'Is there something I should know, Julian?'

'Oh yes, babe. There certainly is.'

'Something I should know before we go in?'

'They didn't tell you?' he sniggered.

We were getting within earshot of the mourners now, so my desperation was squeezed out between gritted teeth. 'No they didn't tell me, but I think *you* should fucking well tell me right now!'

Julian was enjoying himself. 'He was doing time when he died.'

'OK. For what?'

'For drugging and raping his little niece.'

If 'My Way' had been playing already it would have come to an abrupt halt with the scratch of a stylus.

'So you're telling me thirty seconds before I'm about to lead a funeral that the bloke we're burying, the bloke I'm about to eulogise, was a paedophile?'

Julian nodded, his face purple with pent up laughter.

'You bastard,' I whispered. We were at the crem doors now. 'If you are able, please stand,' I said aloud to the congregation trying to be inclusive to the disabled, although this could have included any number of family members who were already too pissed to get up.

No wonder you weren't forthcoming, I thought, as I walked down the aisle taking in the family. No wonder you didn't fancy elaborating on the youth club, I winced to myself. *He was generous with his time. Helping the youth.* I cringed at the words written on the notes in my pocket.

'Dave would have a hard-on in his coffin right now if he could see how fit the priest is,' I heard one of the congregation mutter.

'Would he though, since I'm not twelve?' I said to myself wryly. Then, 'Please, God,' I muttered, 'please don't let me fuck this up. Guide me! Let me say the right things. Let me be sensitive to those he hurt and yet let me feel forgiveness for Dave too.'

Yes, forgiveness. It is fundamental to Christianity. And it is one of the greatest tenets of the faith; one of the greatest attributes a human being can possess. Before Jesus died – spoiler alert! Yes, Jesus dies in the end – he was crucified with two other men. Both were criminals. They are not actually named in the Bible, but let's call them Bob and Fred. In the gospel of Luke, we are told how Bob, along with many onlookers, mocks Jesus as the three of them hang there dying.

'If you're the son of God then why don't you save yourself?' he taunts. 'And save us while you're about it!'

But his mate Fred doesn't join in. In fact he has a go at Bob for being such a dick. 'We are being punished for what we've done, Bob, but this man has done nothing wrong.'

Fred then turns to Jesus and says, 'Please remember me when you come into your kingdom.'

Jesus replies, 'Truly I tell you, today you will be with me in paradise.'

Jesus forgives Fred. He even forgives those onlookers that mock him and coldly divide his clothes up among themselves by casting lots. 'Forgive them, Father, for they know not what they do.'

If we want forgiveness when our time comes, then we must be forgiving too. And for me that had to include Dave.

I cleared my throat which was unusually dry. 'I am the resurrection and the life, says the Lord. Those who believe in me, even though they die, will live, and everyone who lives and believes in me will never die,' I said as the coffin was placed in position at the front and Jim and Kurt congratulated themselves on a job well done. 'The steadfast love of the Lord never ceases. His mercies never come to an end, they are new every morning – *lucky for you, Dave.*' Obviously I didn't say those last few words out loud, but it was a close shave.

This forgiveness lark is easier said than done. People often say being a Christian is easy. It's the perfect way to get you off the hook, they say, to abrogate responsibility, put it all in God's hands – you must be fucking joking.

Julian and the bearers bowed at the coffin and took their seats at the back. I insisted they stay to help with the singing of the hymns, otherwise, as usual, it would be like listening to Rylan Clark audition for *X Factor*. The family had finally decided on ATB&B (that's 'All Things Bright And Beautiful' to the unhip). They said it was appropriate because Dave liked gardening, but we all knew, since they weren't exactly regulars at church, it was the only hymn they could remember from school.

'Please be seated,' I said as I came to the lectern. And, after the avalanche of bums onto seats and the inevitable fidgeting and coughing had diminished, I took a deep breath and began. 'Good morning and welcome to this funeral ceremony of farewell and thanksgiving to a... loved family member and friend, to Dave. It is a... privilege for me to welcome you all here today.' *You can do it*, I told myself. 'We are meeting here this morning to honour the life of Dave. A funeral ceremony is an opportunity to join in taking leave of someone we have loved and... respected, but it is so much more than that.' *You're telling me!* 'Today it is a celebration of his...' the notes said marvellous life '... a life we can only marvel at; his... unique,' always a handy adjective to have in reserve, 'and quirky personality, and it's a time to comfort one another, friends and family who have all been drawn together by his death.'

I thought things were going OK. And as I went on I was so relieved that I had managed to navigate the minefield of this eulogy that I let my guard down on the home stretch and said, 'And although Dave is no longer with us, we can rest assured that he continues to live on through the lives of all those he touched.'

I saw Andrea pale and Sonia plant her long red nails into Jim's knee.

Fuck.

I was aware of Julian on the back row, rolling about and clutching his stomach as if he had just been shot in it. His face looked like a giant bruise now as he tried desperately to contain an explosion of laughter, so I glared at him until he got up and sneaked out. The doors closed behind him just as the first guffaw burst out of him and ricocheted around the walls of the usually peaceful garden of remembrance.

TWENTY-TWO

Spencer and I loved a party and – although I detest the whole trick or treat bullshit and if any one comes knocking on my door I hand them a Bible, not sweets – Halloween was a great excuse for one.

'A priest celebrating Halloween?' Diana said when I invited her after the service the Sunday before. Diana was the organist at St Augustine's, one of my churches. She was about one hundred and fifty years old and had apparently staved off death by pickling herself from the inside with a constant flow of alcohol. She stank like a bottle of Harveys Bristol Cream and loved playing at weddings because it gave her an excuse to congratulate all the guests with a full kiss on the lips from her toothless mouth. Even though she could be a complete pain in the arse, there was something deliciously naughty about her – I guess it takes one to know one.

'Of course,' I explained. 'It's a Christian festival, Di. Halloween is a contraction of All Hallows' Eve and it begins the observance of Allhallows tide, the time in the church's year when we remember all the departed, including the martyrs and the saints, otherwise known as hallows.'

'Ooh,' Diana squeaked. 'I never knew that. I just thought it was a good excuse for people to act like wankers and blame it on the devil.' She mused on this for a brief moment then said, 'Some people said you'd be hopeless, being a slip of a girl and that, but you seem to know your stuff.'

After swallowing the bile that raised in me, I smiled and said, 'So are you coming?'

'To your party?'

I nodded as patiently as I could.

'Will there be booze?'

'Plenty.'

Di's eyes lit up. And then I landed the decisive blow. 'Sherry too.'

'Well, of course I'll be there,' Di said and staggered off to retrieve her shopping from under the organ.

I invited Erin and Julian too. I'd forgiven him for taking the piss so brutally out of me at Dave's funeral. Besides, funeral directors always seemed to be more fun than anyone else in the church. And, among many other guests, who now filled the manse, I'd also invited Hannah and Natalie, two of the girls from my pole fitness class, and it wasn't long before we were having a pole-off upstairs. It was lit.

Spencer and the other male guests including Hannah's partner Larry, soon sniffed what was going on and stood around in the pole room ogling – which was fine by me. But then, men being men, they began to insist that they could do better on the pole without ever having had a lesson in their lives. Spencer was first to try to copy the moves we girls had done.

He cracked a rib in the process.

Later, I was in the kitchen holding a bag of frozen peas to Spencer's torso.

'I fell over in the bath a few years back,' Di said, watching Spencer and me as if she was watching a particularly shit act on *Britain's Got Talent*. 'Broke my hip. Didn't have a clue I'd done it for weeks.'

The advantages of being permanently pissed, I thought, before being distracted from nursing my husband by some groans coming from outside. Another man nursing his wounds from the pole room, perhaps? I followed the sounds out to the front garden where I found Natalie and Hannah stark naked under my begonias, clit to clit, having a fine old time. I couldn't blame Natalie. Hannah was stunning. I'd snogged her at a few parties and, in a hot tub once, well... let's just say our hands might have wandered. Spencer didn't mind of course, because I was playing with a girl. Had it been with another bloke things would have been different. The general rule of thumb was: hetero's a no-no, homo's a go-go.

'Everything all right?' Di's voice came from the front door, her nose as sharp as a Beagle's when it came to sniffing out trouble.

'Yes, yes,' I said, ushering her inside. She may be well preserved but the sight of these scissor sisters here might well finish her off at last.

Turning back to the girls I hissed, 'This is a church house.' I looked up and down the street praying that no one had seen the girl-on-girl action on my lawn as they passed by on their way back from a nice meal at the Harvester (if that's not an oxymoron).

Natalie and Hannah looked up at me, breathless and contrite.

'So get inside! And use my bed to have sex, not the garden,' I said admiring their naked forms.

We all know the church in general has a reputation for being sexually repressed – and we've all seen in the Catholic Church how that can turn out. The church is often scandalised by the human form in all its naked glory. We think of Adam and Eve, having eaten from the Tree of Knowledge, becoming aware of their bodies for the first time and covering up their erstwhile public parts with fig leaves in shame. But that's not what the Bible actually says. This tale has been spun by theologians like Augustine of Hippo, the fifth century bishop who used this moment in the Bible to expound the dangers of the flesh. He was a reformed womaniser himself, of course. Nothing worse than a reformed anything. They've had their fun, then decide that no one else is allowed theirs – St Paul being a case in point.

But there's nothing in the Bible to suggest that Adam and Eve covering their genitals was related to sexual knowledge or their distaste for it. They're not doing this because of sexualised self-corruption but in fact because of their newfound knowledge, which drives them to create culture – clothes being the first rung on that ladder. God even makes them more clothes from leather while he says to his heavenly gang, 'Adam and Eve have now become like one of us in their knowledge.' And, of course, we are told he created them 'in his image' in the first place. That's why many Greco-

Roman influenced depictions of Christ and God show a naked and very human form.

'The Risen Christ' is a masterpiece of Renaissance spirituality sculpted from marble by Michelangelo. In the original version finished in the early 1520s (and these days hidden away behind the walls of a monastery in the small Italian town of Bassano Romano) Christ is almost seven feet tall holding upright the cross on which he was killed. His body is athletic, burly even, and it is also magnificently naked. His penis is there for all to see. Yes, Jesus had genitals. What did you think this human looked like under his loincloth, Action Man? This first version was abandoned by Michelangelo when he discovered imperfections in the marble. So he began again and the second version still stands in its originally intended spot in Rome. However, later in 1546, this one had a gaudy bronze loincloth tacked on over the genitals. It's a ridiculous addition. Jesus looks like he's been given one of those dodgy C-strings to wear, those half-schlong-thongs worn by TOWIE types on the beaches of Marbella.

And the nether regions revisionism didn't stop there. In 1565 some gaudy drapery was painted over the junk of the writhing nude figures in Michelangelo's once magnificent 'Last Judgement' on the ceiling of the Sistine Chapel, which only serves to make them look like they're having a fight in a curtain shop.

The censoring of Michelangelo's work was just one of the Counter-Reformation strategies adopted by bishops in the wake of the Council of Trent in the mid-sixteenth century to tackle what was thought to be the profanity of frontal nudity in Christian art. Michelangelo was of course simply celebrating the humanity of the divine Christ, but for those meddling bishops the genitals were morally dangerous – but then they would think that, wouldn't they, since they so often used theirs for such morally dubious purposes.

Even God himself is described in the Bible by Ezekiel (Chapter 1) as a corporal being, 'like that of a man'. God

114

comes to Ezekiel in a vision. In many translations of the Bible you will hear Ezekiel describe God's glowing body from the waist up and how from the waist down it was like fire. Reminds me of how I feel about Spencer. But the original Hebrew word used here is אִיבְרֵי הַמִין which doesn't actually mean waist at all, but genitals. The God of the Hebrew Bible – or Yahweh – is often described in heavily masculine and phallic terminology. Yahweh had no problem with letting it all hang out. This God is embroiled with sexuality. Because there's nothing wrong with sex. Sex is the meaning of life – not 42, as Douglas Adams might have you think. Without sex we wouldn't be here. And that is true for the entire human race, for the whole of history. We have to deal with and get over the 'shocking' idea that Jesus must be the product of sex too and that, indeed, he had the tools to have sex himself should he so wish. Even if he was celibate – poor sod – how else would he take a leak?

The girls grinned and rushed inside to continue what they'd started.

As I went back through the front door Di was still there.

'Having sex, were they?' she said. 'Too cold out there for it,' she nodded.

I nodded too.

'I was a lesbian once,' she said wistfully. 'Well, I think I was. I can't quite remember.'

The disadvantages of being permanently pissed, I thought.

Larry danced into the hallway just then having triumphed at apple bobbing in the lounge.

'Where's Hannah?' he asked me through his grin.

'She's upstairs being a lesbian,' Di cut in.

Larry's face dropped and he shot up to the bedroom. I gave Di an *I'm disappointed in you* look and trudged up the stairs in order to try and help minimise the damage (to my bedroom as well as anyone's emotions).

But when I poked my head into the room, I saw both Hannah and Natalie bobbing for something greater than apples and a huge grin on Larry's face.

TWENTY-THREE

Another day, another funeral. And there are plenty of them in these pages mainly because I think they're more important than weddings. As a minister I am almost part of the window dressing of a wedding by the time the big day comes. You can always tell how important the church service is to a couple by whether they ask you to be in the photographs outside. Most of the time it's, 'Do you mind? You're in the way,' but if you're asked to say cheese then you know the service meant something more to them than playing princess.

At a funeral I feel a huge responsibility; one which I am honoured to bear. These are heart-wrenching and vulnerable times for the grieving and they often look to a priest to be steadfast when they are unsteady, to be compassionate when they might be angry. It is an enormously complex time and a huge moment of transition. It is when I am able to help ease that burden at such a time that my vocation seems to have the greatest meaning.

Eric was eighty-six years old and a regular at church every Sunday. A total gent. Always offering to lend a hand, a smile for everyone. He looked like a Pixar version of an old man – always wore a tie, thick glasses, no teeth and his small hunched frame was propped up by a walking stick – which made you want to cuddle him at the best of times. So it was shocking to see his kind eyes red with emotion, tears soaking his jowls, and to hear the little sobs popping out from behind the liver-spotted hand he held over his mouth one Sunday as the service came to an end.

When everyone had gone, I joined him on the pew he couldn't seem to prise himself out of.

'Eric? Eric, what's the matter?' I said putting an arm around him.

As priests, we are not supposed to initiate any kind of physical contact, but sometimes you have to say bollocks to the rules. This man needed a hug and not to initiate physical contact then would've been neglectful, in my opinion.

'I... I don't... I can't... They won't...' He shook his head.

'Take your time. I'm here for you.'

'It's OK,' he said eventually. 'Ignore me. I'm being silly. I'm sorry,' he said, looking embarrassed now.

'You're not OK, Eric and it's not silly,' I said as he staggered to his feet and edged out of the pew, but I could see he wasn't able or willing to articulate what was going on right now. 'I'll come and see you tomorrow,' I told him.

He didn't agree, but he didn't disagree. So the next morning I was on his doorstep as early as I thought it appropriate to be.

When he answered the door his eyes were pregnant with tears. 'Hello, my dear,' he said and broke down again.

He allowed me to usher him inside, then, for a change, I was the one making the tea, which he accepted gratefully and, like the magic potion it is, it helped him to compose himself enough to speak.

'My partner Beryl... died,' he said, still struggling with the enormity and other-worldliness of such a statement. 'Two weeks ago.'

'Oh, Eric. I am so sorry,' I said, giving him the hug he clearly needed. 'No wonder you are upset.'

'Well, yes. I still can't quite believe it's true that she's gone. But the worst of it is, Beryl's family won't let me go to her funeral.'

'What?' I said, sitting back. I couldn't believe what I was hearing. 'Why on earth not? She's your partner.'

'Yes, for over twenty years,' Eric found his handkerchief and dabbed at his nose. 'But when we first met, we were both married to other people.' He looked at me sheepishly.

'Go on,' I said.

'We had an affair.'

I nodded only, making sure my face expressed no judgement, willing him to carry on.

'Gosh, she was a beauty,' he said, his eyes glazing over with the memory. 'I was in a bar in Soho, a work thing with a bunch of other doctors just before the war, when I first spotted her. She was so pretty that every man in the room was after her, but I didn't even have the guts to speak to her. Eventually, she came over and chatted me up, can you believe it?' he chuckled. 'A woman making the first move!'

I smiled. Yes, actually, I could believe it.

'She told me after that it was because she'd had one too many glasses of port. "Every other boy here has asked me to dance tonight. Every other boy has flirted with me, except you," she said. And I said – I remember it just like it was yesterday – I said, "I'm not really one for dancing... nor for flirting." And then she looked a bit put out, you know, so I explained it wasn't that she wasn't attractive, far from it, but that it was me; I wasn't that confident. And she said, "Your friend over there told me you're a great surgeon, so you can't tell me you don't have confidence." "Ah!" I said. "Confidence in medicine is not the same as confidence in situations like this." And then she cocked her head, a bit like you're doing right now, so I told her there are hundreds of text books that tell you exactly what to do when it comes to medicine. All you have to do is memorise the facts. And she came back with, "But there's plenty of books that tell you what to do in these situations too." "Really?" I said. "Which ones? I'd love to read them." "*Romeo and Juliet*," she said without hesitation. "Indeed," I said, "but look how that ends," I parried playfully. "*Gone with the Wind*," she said. "*Madame Bovary*." So I said, "That's the one about the woman who reads too many books about love and ends up ruining her life, isn't it?" And she slapped me gently on my chest – it was the most wonderful sensation; the first time she ever touched me. "*Pride and Prejudice*," she added and kept her hand there as she reeled off more of the world's most famous love stories. I was captivated. Her dark eyes were so full of adventure, her high cheekbones bursting with mischief, and, with all I already knew about anatomy, it was the perfect example to me of why there had to be more to life than flesh, blood and bone. Why I believed in God.'

I knew exactly what he meant.

'We danced. I was rubbish. Stepped on her toe. She said it didn't matter and I started to enjoy knowing that all the men in the room were envious of me. And then I started to worry. What if one of these men came now and stole her away from me with their social confidence, their Rhett Butler boldness, their Mr Darcy dash? And yet I should not have even been thinking that way. I was married, for pity's sake. And so was she. But the gears of my heart had shifted, the parameters of my world widened, the focus I had always had on my work and home was now disturbed and suddenly everything got a lot more complicated. Deliciously complicated.' He came back from his memories and blinked at me as if he had just woken from a dream. 'You must think me awful.'

I shook my head. 'That was beautiful.'

So he went on, 'Our affair didn't go on for that many months before we were both wracked with guilt. We decided we had to come clean to our spouses. We were both Christians. Well, Beryl was the kind who went to church at Christmas; Easter, at a push. But we both believed in marriage. We had not taken our vows lightly. We had to try to make our marriages work. And so we did. And then twenty-five years ago, my wife died and a few years later Beryl's husband died. Please don't think we were waiting for that day. We weren't, but when it came, we both found each other again when she coincidentally moved into my street, as if it was always meant to be. We both had a good few more wrinkles than when we first met, to say the least, so it wasn't merely a physical thing, you understand. She was the love of my life. And I realise now she was since that first time I saw her in Soho.' He began to sob again. 'But Beryl's family never forgave me for the affair and now they've banned me from her funeral.'

'But you're her husband. They can't.'

He shook his head. 'We never married. Out of some sort of respect to our deceased spouses.'

'What a load of bollocks,' I said.

This sobered Eric up.

119

'Not you not getting married,' I clarified. 'You being barred from the funeral. Sorry, Eric, but this is wrong. When is it?'

'The funeral? Today. This morning,' he groaned, as he saw his chance to say goodbye slipping through his fingers.

'Come on then!' I stood up. 'Grab your coat!'

'I beg your pardon?' He blinked up at me like a child waking.

'We're going to that fucking funeral. You have as much right to say goodbye to her as they do.'

TWENTY-FOUR

The funeral service was taking place at a church in another parish. It had just begun when we got there. Everyone was focused on the priest beginning the eulogy so we were able to slip into the pew at the back. I put an arm protectively around Eric and he quietly wept on my shoulder throughout, soaking my shirt with his tears.

During a hymn – I can't remember which it was, but it wasn't ATB&B, Beryl had more taste than that – one of Beryl's relatives spotted Eric and slunk over to us.

'Excuse me,' she hissed. She was around my age, I suspected, so she had to be Beryl's granddaughter. 'You were told you can't be here.'

'Yes, yes,' Eric said, 'I'm sorry. We'll go. I don't want to make a scene.'

'Woah there, cowgirl,' I whispered to the daughter. 'I understand this is a terribly upsetting time for you. Funerals are all about *closure*.' I sounded like a soapy '90s US drama, which I thought at her age she would appreciate. 'They are a rite of passage, which you need. But Eric also needs to take that rite. And that rite is his right, if you know what I mean.'

'Well, he's banned,' she snapped. 'And who the hell are you, anyway?'

I opened my coat, like Superman before he slips into a phone box, to reveal my dog collar. 'A funeral is a public act of worship and no one can be banned, if you want me to get all technical on your arse. Now please go and sit down. The only person making a scene here is you. Beryl wouldn't want that, would she? Don't worry, we'll be gone by the time everyone's finished slaughtering this hymn.'

She skulked back to her pew, poor girl. I felt sorry for her, but I felt sorry for everyone grieving for Beryl right then. Including, of course, the love of her life.

Affairs are unfortunate, but they happen. A lot. Because you cannot help who you fall in love with. For those caught in the traps of affairs it is torture. There is pain all around.

121

Nobody ever wins. But as ministers we must offer those involved, on every side, guidance through the mire, not condemnation.

TWENTY-FIVE

Once a month part of my duties was to go into the local retirement home for the elderly. You've got to love the elderly! They tell it how it is. Generally, they don't suffer fools. They know the clock is ticking for them and they don't have time for any nonsense. The old folks I would visit were born in or just after the Second World War. Most of them remember what it was like to not have central heating or an inside loo. Some remember when polio and TB could kill you, and electricity was a luxury. Some recall bombs raining down on them night after night and having to sleep in their mother's arms in an underground shelter while their father fought Hitler, not knowing if he'd ever return. Thus they tend not to cry over spilt milk, and yet, if you give them a dairy substitute they'll look at you like you just served them sheep's testicles.

Grace was one such baby boomer who lived in Happy Ending Villas. She was being served her lunch when I came into the common room to set up the service with Erin. She had a voice like a broken exhaust pipe and looked as if she was permanently sucking on one too.

'Is this my lunch?' she said to the care assistant as he put a plate before her.

'Yes, Grace. Shepherd's pie.'

'Did I tell you how much I liked this when we had it last week?'

'No,' the assistant said expectantly. 'I don't think so.'

'Then why are you serving me this crap again?' Grace said looking despairing at the anaemic thing on her plate.

It's often tough to pitch these gigs. I can't churn out the usual sermon, encouraging people to turn their lives around, and be the change they want to see – elderly dog new tricks and all that. But equally I can't harp on about death all the time. I mean, that would just be rubbing it in, wouldn't it? So I try to keep it upbeat and positive, with plenty of singing, although dear old Jean will start singing every time I open my mouth to speak, so I usually ask Erin to sit next to her to rein her in. On this occasion, Erin tried to sit in the empty chair to Jean's left, but Edna, sitting on the other side of the empty chair, stopped her.

'Someone's sitting there,' Edna said politely but firmly.

'Oh, I'm sorry,' Erin said. 'Who?' She looked around the room to see if anyone needed assistance finding this seat.

'My Arthur,' Edna smiled.

Erin and I didn't see any blokes who were not seated, and Edna didn't look concerned, so I got started, as did Jean with the first hymn prematurely.

Erin sat on the other side of Jean and told her to hold her horses while I banged on for no more than fifteen minutes. I didn't want to go on too long. Time was of the essence to these people. Besides, if I tried to compete with *Bargain Hunt* I knew I would lose.

Afterwards, I like to chat to the residents before they disperse. While I was congratulating Jean on yet another enthusiastic participation in the hymns, I heard the not so welcome vocal stylings of Grace from behind me.

'Did you know I was a lay preacher?' she rasped.

I turned. 'Really?' I said, trying not to sound too surprised.

'Seventy years,' Grace nodded self-approvingly.

'You were a lay preacher for seventy years?' I gasped. 'That's amazing. I hope I can be a priest for at least half that long. Although, between you and me,' I said, enjoying finding some common ground with Grace, whose name didn't seem so ironic any longer, 'there are plenty of people in the church who would like to get rid of me. Particularly the men.'

'Ah! I understand,' my suffragist sister said knowingly, before adding, 'And I don't blame them if you continue to preach like that.' She looked at me like she looked at the minced cow on her plate earlier and shuffled away.

As I recovered from that one star review, I spotted that the seat next to Edna was still not filled, so I went over and asked, 'What happened to your Arthur?' hoping he hadn't had a fall or something in their room.

'Oh, he died three years ago,' she smiled.

Every time there was a service, Edna saved that seat for Arthur.

That night in bed I clung onto Spencer for dear life.

TWENTY-SIX

Another Sunday sermon ended with a mic drop moment. No, this wasn't me arrogantly thinking I'd knocked it out of the park; I'd handed my lapel mic and pack to Erin and she'd literally dropped it.

'Sorry, Reverend,' she said. 'A little distracted today.'

'No need to call me Reverend, Erin,' I said, then added quietly, 'Need to talk about anything? Something worrying you?'

'No, no, everything is fine actually. It's just that...' She looked up at the crucifix above the altar and ushered me out of the church through a side door. And once she thought we were safely out of earshot of Christ, she whispered. 'I've met a boy. I mean, a man. I'm not a... I've met a lovely gentleman and we're having lots of S... E... X.' Her lips moved like a character from *Wallace & Gromit* as she tried to say the letters without saying them.

'That's wonderful, Erin. I'm so happy for you. And don't worry. Jesus would be happy to hear about it too,' I said, leading her round to the front doors, through which the congregation was now filing out, so I could say goodbye to them.

'Really?' Erin hissed.

'Of course. How do you think he was conceived in the first place? Immaculate conception?' I laughed.

Erin was confused, but there was no time to explain now.

'Thank you, Reverend,' said Sue from the village shop as she emerged with her husband Ralph. He was on the parish council and liked to think of himself as a bit of a squire, although the local Londis was hardly a country estate.

'Always inspiring, isn't she?' said Ralph to his wife, patting me on the arse.

What's that saying? The first time is an accident, the second is a choice. This was the second time Ralph had groped me. Enough was enough.

'Excuse me,' I said. 'Did you used to touch up the former priest here?'

If we'd been in the Wild West nothing would have moved right then except for some tumbleweed blowing by as the church bell tolled once.

Sue reddened and I felt sorry for her, but I couldn't let her slimy spouse get away with it.

Ralph babbled for a moment then managed to say, 'Touch up? Who touched anyone up?' He laughed as his eyes darted around the congregation filing out around us.

'You patted me on my bottom,' I said calmly. 'Just then. And not for the first time. Did you do that to the former priest here?'

'To Brian? No, no, of course not,' Ralph said as if the idea disgusted him.

'Then why would you do it to me?' I said, cocking my head as if deep in thought.

'Well…' he said, his round head resembling a beetroot more with every excruciating second.

Sue rushed off. I dropped an imaginary mic this time. And Ralph hurried after his long-suffering wife.

Ralph passed away a few months later. Surprisingly, Sue decided not to flush his ashes down the toilet, but to have them ceremonially buried in the garden of remembrance with me officiating.

Julian brought the ashes in a container and a few close family members huddled around a rose bush in the garden where the ashes were to be poured. By then I had done plenty of burials and cremations but not too many burials of ashes, and I made the rooky mistake of standing downwind as Julian emptied the little box. The crushed remains of Ralph's bones (for that is all ashes are) flew into my face, my hair and my open prayer book. As much as I wanted to squeal and run about the place, I kept my composure – Sue didn't need to see me spitting and shaking out my hair at a time like this – and when the brief ceremony was over, I sloped off into a back room at the crematorium and brushed that man right out of my hair. Ashes were lodged in the crevice between the open pages of the prayer book too, so I stepped outside and I huffed and I puffed until the pages were Ralph-free.

'You must be happy now, Ralph, old boy,' I said wryly to the air. 'At last you got a blow job from me.'

Back in the present, I was still bidding farewell to the congregation.

'Bye, Ray,' I beamed at the young man next through the doors. 'Will you be at the anniversary lunch this year?'

'Yeah, yeah. I'll be there,' Ray said.

'Why don't you bring Trudy?'

He nodded. 'I'll ask her,' he said without much hope in his eyes. Trudy wasn't a churchgoer.

'Fab!' I said. 'Need some young blood there.' I nudged him conspiratorially.

He giggled politely at the potty priest and waved as he went.

'Eric!' I said as he came out after them. 'How are you?' It had been a few months since the funeral.

'Bearing up, my dear. Bearing up,' he smiled bravely, though his eyes betrayed the smile.

So I said brightly, 'I'm coming to make you a cuppa tomorrow morning, OK?'

'OK,' he said.

*

The next morning ensconced on his sumptuous sofa, Earl Grey in hand, Eric opened up.

'Every time something comes round, you know, an event, for the first time since she... died. My birthday. Valentine's Day. I dread it. My kids try to do something nice, bless them, but it just magnifies the fact that she's missing. On her birthday I was doing some DIY. The drainpipe needed fixing. I'd been putting it off forever. Anyway, when I finally got on with it, I was so absorbed that I almost forgot what day it was. But Facebook must have sent all my friends and family notification of her birthday and I got inundated with sympathetic messages. It's so sweet of them, but it actually just reminds me of what I've lost.'

'It's hard to pull off,' I said, 'but I guess the trick is not to mourn for what you've lost, but to celebrate all those years you had together. The miracle of the time you had.'

'Miracle?' he asked, blinking away the tears welling in his eyes.

'Yes. The miracle of that very first meeting. Think about it! What if you hadn't gone out that night with your workmates? What if you had decided not to bother and gone home instead? What if one of your mates had persuaded you all to go to the club across the street from the bar you ended up in? You could have been metres away from Beryl but never actually in the same room. What if you'd never worked at that hospital in London but taken a job nearer here? Of all the cities you could've chosen, you chose London, of all the places in London, you went out in Soho, and of all the streets in Soho to go to, you went to that street and that bar, and there of all nights was Beryl. What if her friend had twisted her ankle on the way to that bar and they ended up in A&E all night? A&E in your hospital while you were in the bar?'

'My gosh,' Eric breathed the words as the infinite possibilities which could have led to them not ever meeting mushroomed in his mind.

'But when you were in that bar, somehow you fell into each other's orbit and danced. And despite it not being the right time even then, you still danced your dance together for the last twenty magical years.'

Eric sniffed loudly and steepled his fingers before his lips for a long moment. Then he nodded and looked at me with eyes which Beryl was lucky to be the apple of.

'We used to go out a lot and do things together,' he said. 'We'd go to stately homes, or out for a meal, or to the cinema.'

I nodded, thinking how lucky I was to have Spencer to do those things with.

'And now I don't go anywhere. I mean, I *could*. But I don't want to. I don't want to go alone. Where's the fun in that?'

I squeezed his hand then a thought occurred to me. 'Was there something you were thinking about doing recently that you didn't do because of that feeling?' I asked.

'Well,' he blushed a little, 'we liked James Bond films. I suppose I liked them more than she did, but she always suggested it every time a new one came out. We'd buy popcorn. And chocolate. Make pigs of ourselves.'

'Sounds great,' I smiled. The chocolate and the popcorn. Not so sure about the chauvinist secret agent, but this wasn't about me.

'There's a new one out now,' Eric continued. 'When I saw the advert on TV I was just about to turn to Beryl and suggest we go. But in the same split second my heart fell into my boots as I remembered she wasn't... she didn't exist anymore.'

'Physically yes, but you know...'

'Yes, I know.' He gave me the smile he thought I wanted to see. 'Everyone tells me she's in a better place now. But I can't help thinking this isn't true. Not for her. If Beryl is somehow conscious, aware, in spirit, then I know she'd be upset at being separated from her family, from me. She loved life and she loved people so so much, she hated feeling left out. And now she would feel left out. Eternally. Which would be like Hell to her. I can't stand that thought. I can't accept that is a possibility. So I have to believe she just ceased to exist. Completely. Mind and body. Or at least that she is sleeping dreamlessly forever.'

I could feel Eric shuffling along the ledge of despair. I needed to coax him back through the window and into the safety of the room.

'Don't think of her as existing in some other realm distant from you. You won't forget her, will you? You won't stop thinking about the good times or erase her from your memory? So she will always remain a part of you and live

130

inside of you because of the love you shared with each other.'

Eric squeezed his own hand as if he was trying to feel Beryl's touch there.

'What we know about death, as you well know, *Dr* Samuels, is really limited. Because we are not dead. As theologians and as doctors we have some theories and even some evidence, but at the end of the day, we just don't know. What I find helpful is knowing that the God that you and I believe in is bigger than all of this pain, all of the family problems and that hate and the separation you feel. I believe that God is bigger than all of this because this world is so screwed up and broken.'

Eric nodded his amen to that.

'I don't want a replica of what's going on here somewhere else. I want something literally beyond my imagination. For me, God's love has the capacity to encompass the very real and tangible love you and Beryl had. That love was not in vain. You can't help who you fall in love with. God knows that because God fell in love with me, poor sod. And you.'

Eric's cheeks rose with a smile and wrung a single tear from each eye.

'You are loved, Eric Samuels. You are treasured. God holds your pain and weeps when you are weeping. God loves Beryl just as much as you do, perhaps more so. God has a place in his heart which has the capacity for all of that pain and love way beyond anything we can possibly imagine. I have to believe that. And I hope you do too.'

'Thank you,' Eric mouthed, wiping at his eyes.

'So let's go!' I said jumping up.

'Beg your pardon, my love?'

'I want to see the new James Bond too,' I lied. 'But Spencer doesn't like them. So I've got no one to go with either. Will you come with me?'

Eric looked at me with an amused suspicion as I hopped about the room with excitement.

'Please?'

When he eventually agreed, there was such a sense of relief in the room, we both laughed loudly for a moment, before Eric clapped his hand over his mouth.

'Are you OK, Eric?'

'I feel so… self-conscious. For laughing. As if I shouldn't really have been laughing. As if it is wrong to laugh. As if I should have waited for Beryl to be here before I laughed. So she didn't miss out.'

'Just think how annoyed she would be with you if she saw you sitting in here on your own day after day and never smiling,' I said, playfully scolding him.

He nodded and smiled coyly. 'She always said how much she liked my smile. When I still had my teeth, of course.'

I looked at this man and his cathedral of a heart and I wanted to fill it with rhapsodies, not dirges.

'Do you mind if I invite some other friends along?' I asked.

'Who do you have in mind?' he said.

TWENTY-SEVEN

'Well, this is exciting, isn't it?' Di shouted from the back of my BMW 4 series convertible. 'I feel like I'm in a James Bond movie already in this thing.'

Di was shouting because I'd put the top down and the wind was rushing through our ears as I drove into town. It wasn't quite warm enough to have the top down – when is it warm enough to have the top down in England? – but I was partly showing off, partly getting everyone pumped up and, most importantly, letting in enough fresh air so we didn't all pass out on Di's sherry breath.

Eric rode up front with me. Linda was in the back with Di. Linda was the wife of Liam, the Spurs supporter and regular at The Moon and Stars pub for forty years, who we buried not that many months before Beryl's funeral. Despite her not giving 'a toss' about the religious side of Liam's funeral, I gave a toss about her and admired her honesty. I also knew that the best way I could minister to Eric, having never lost the love of my life, was to get him talking with someone who had. He needed to know he wasn't alone in his feelings and so, for that matter, did Linda.

I'm not sure if Di had a husband, a wife or was a widow. She never talked about it. Actually, I'm not sure how she managed to get in on this trip. I think she overheard me telling Eric that we would be going to one of those upmarket Everyman cinemas where you sit in comfy sofas and the waiters bring you booze. She was sold and invited herself.

'Is it included with the ticket?' Di asked as we took our seats, Di and me in one sofa, Eric and Linda in the next.

'No, Di, you have to pay for what you drink and eat,' I said before she ordered everything on the menu.

'Oh,' she wilted slightly, but when the waiter walked past, she collared him and said, 'Lemonade, please.'

'Di?' I said. 'Are you OK?'

'Fine thanks.'

'If you're worried about the cost I'll—'

'No. I've... um... just got a little dose of the runs. A lemonade should settle my tummy.'

'Oh, OK,' I said, scanning the room for the toilet sign, should an emergency arise. 'Eric?'

'Ooh, well, how about a red wine? House is fine,' he said. His eyes sparkled in the light of the adverts playing on the screen.

'Linda?'

'Stout?'

The young waiter frowned.

'Like a Guinness?' I clarified.

'Yeah, that'll do. Half a Guinness,' she said.

'Anyone for popcorn?' Eric said, shaking a great bucket of the stuff at us.

'Don't mind if I do,' Linda said, scooping out a handful.

'No thank you,' Di said.

'Go on!' Eric smiled. 'There's no way I can get through this by my—' he pretended to be distracted by the advert for Omega watches playing on the screen as the words *by myself* threatened to remind him that, although he was here with three other people, he was essentially, now, on his own. That popcorn would have been shared with Beryl before. There would have been no discussion about it. No offering needed. Everything they had done would have been instinctive, telepathic.

'Go on, Di!' I goaded her, trying to jolt Eric back from wherever he had gone. 'Spoil yourself!'

'Even the smallest popcorn is too big for one, innit?' I heard Linda say quietly to Eric.

'Yes,' he sighed. 'It's funny how you notice that society is made for couples when you're on your own. I mean, look!' he said, gesturing to the screen. 'Buy this car and drive around in it with your partner. Buy this paint and paint your house with your boyfriend. Buy this bag of crisps for sharing in front of the television with your wife.'

'Load of old balls, innit?' Linda said.

Eric smiled, enjoying her turn of phrase. 'Couldn't have put it better myself.'

'Rubs it in, dunnit? Makes you remember how lonely you are.'

'How long has it been for you?' Eric said, anxious to hear her story.

'A year, just about. You?'

'Three months, two days, thirteen hours,' Eric said immediately.

'Still counting, eh?'

Eric nodded bashfully.

'It does get easier,' Linda said, 'even after a year, but I reckon you don't get over it. You just learn to live with it.' They watched the screen for a moment before Linda added, 'You're a surgeon, aincha?'

Eric nodded, not sure of where she was going with this.

'Amputated anything?'

'A leg or two,' he smiled.

'Those patients'll never be the same again. But they work round it, don't they?'

'They do,' he smiled gratefully.

Just then the waiter appeared and handed out the drinks.

'Thanks awfully,' Di said with suspiciously excessive politeness. And when the waiter had disappeared again, she downed the lemonade and pulled a bottle of sherry out of her bag. 'Buggered if I'm paying those prices,' she said, refilling the lemonade glass with the beverage she really wanted.

'Cheers to you!' Eric laughed, clinking his glass with Di's. 'And you,' he said to Linda. 'And you,' he said to me with a wink, as the lights went down and Daniel Craig shot across the screen in a fast sports car.

*

As much as I could decry the lame attempts to empower the female characters in the movie and the efforts to distract us from the inherent sexism in this franchise with greater stunts, crazier gadgets and bigger explosions, I have to admit I felt a little thrilled by the thriller we'd just seen and I fired up my Beemer just as 007 had revved up his.

'I'm with Bond on fast cars,' I said to my passengers. 'I guess it's not all about compensating for a small penis.'

Linda cackled at the priest saying penis, Di whooped as we sped off and Eric held on to the door nervously while laughing with abandon.

The film had ended with Bond losing a loved one. I had cringed as the credits rolled, hoping I hadn't set Eric and Linda back.

'Sorry Eric if...'

But Eric had leant over to me and whispered, 'It's OK. Loss is like learning a new word, you know. You hear it and see it everywhere suddenly. Of course it was always there, but you didn't know the word so you glossed over it. In the same way, when you lose someone you suddenly notice that every bloody song, every book, every film,' he said nodding at the screen, 'involves death somewhere. And why not? There's nothing more powerful, more inevitable.'

As the evening wind rushed through our heads, Linda squealed, 'Hey, Eric, we're you're Bond girls.'

'And one of them is in the driving seat. The way it should be,' I winked at Eric and put my foot down again, pumped by the sensory overload we'd had in the cinema.

'You OK, Di? Bit quiet for you,' I shouted over my shoulder.

'Bloody popcorn,' she slurred. 'Stuck under my dentures.'

'Oops, sorry,' Eric shouted and giggled in my direction.

We were all having a whale of a time – even Di, once she'd popped out her teeth and washed them in the remaining sherry in her bag, which wasn't much – until we were besieged by a blue flashing light coming from behind us.

'Shit,' I said.

'Oh dear,' Eric said.

Linda whooped with delight.

'Was I speeding?' I asked Eric.

'I'm not sure. What's the speed limit here? Must be sixty.'

I smelt my breath. 'Fuck. I've been drinking.'

'Yes, but only one.'

'Two,' I said sheepishly.

Eric looked at me questioningly.

'You didn't see. You were distracted by that Russian spy getting her kit off.'

Linda was cracking up. 'This is great. I don't think I've ever been caught by the fuzz before.'

'I have,' Di shouted and added in utter seriousness, 'So I've shaved down there ever since.'

Linda was cackling now. Having the time of her life. I'm glad she was, in hindsight, but right then I was terrified that I would get arrested and jeopardise my vocation. I pulled over, praying the police car would keep going and that in fact I was just in the way of it trying to nab a real criminal up ahead. But the police car stopped behind me and a gum-chewing policeman got out, who, as it turned out had no gum at all, but just the action of chewing, which I think was supposed to demonstrate how superior and in control he was, but really made him look like he had a bit of KFC stuck between his molars.

'Do you know what speed you were doing back there?' he said as he came to my door.

Was that a trick question? How can you possibly answer that and not look irresponsible? If I answer *yes, I was doing sixty-five*, then, assuming there is a sixty mile an hour speed limit here, I will be flagrantly flouting the law in the mandible grinding face of the law itself. However, if I say no, then doesn't that make me sound like I don't pay attention to what I'm doing and am therefore a danger on the roads who deserves to be locked up? So I plumped for:

'I'm not entirely sure, officer, but if you have one of those thingies... um...'

'Speed recorder? Yes I do. Actually the car is fitted with five cameras and a speed recorder,' he said as if I'd just asked him the girth of his cock and he'd said 'Four inches' – yes, it's girth that matters, boys, not length; a nine inch shaft is only going to feel like my coil consultant destroying her 100% success rate and my cervix to boot.

'Yes,' I said, 'speed recorder. Well, perhaps you could tell me my speed. That would be very helpful,' I waffled while smiling sweetly up at him.

He took in my three OAP passengers. Linda and Di were enjoying their own failure to suppress their giggles.

'He's probably looking for drug dealers,' Linda whispered as only drunk people do – loudly. 'Drug dealers drive BMWs, don't they?'

Thanks, Linda.

Di stuck her hands in the air. 'No cunts on me, drugstable.'

I winced at Di's sozzled spoonerism.

'Been out on the razz, have we?' the copper said with a good dollop of sarcasm.

No would have been the sensible answer and the truth, but there was something about the comment which suddenly raised my hackles. I felt protective of my aged brood, so I replied, 'Are people over the age of seventy not allowed to go out on the *razz*?'

'Eighty,' Di chipped in.

The copper was momentarily embarrassed, but quickly recovered with, 'They are, but you're not if you're driving.' He pulled a breath-testing kit out of somewhere – his arse probably as that was the origin of most things that came out of him – and said, 'Have a blow on that, will you?'

'Ooh,' squealed Linda, 'it's been a while since someone said that to me.'

It was like having Hattie Jacques and Joan Sims in the back of my car and I would have loved every one of their double entendres, intentional or not, had I not been dreading the result of the test. I offered up a quick prayer to God for the all clear – not for the first time after putting my lips round some bloke's equipment (cue Sid James cackling) – and the result was – Hallelujah! – negative. Eric and I both sighed with relief. But the copper hadn't finished.

'Well, for your information, you were going sixty-five back there and the speed limit is sixty.'

I could see that, disappointed he hadn't been able to do me for drinking and driving, he was keen to write me a ticket for speeding, so there was nothing for it but to bring out the big guns. I tossed my hair back, arched my neck and pumped up my chest; that way he could not fail to see, even on this poorly lit road, my clerical shirt and dog collar. You didn't think I was going to use my sex appeal to get away with this, did you? I'm a feminist, for fuck's sake. Besides, my tits aren't big enough.

'I am awfully sorry about that, officer, but…' I gestured to the verge '…if I may have a quick word?'

'You're a vicar?' he said.

'Yes,' I replied through the usual smile of gritted teeth that accompanied that fucking misnomer. Now wasn't the time for pedantry.

'What's a vicar doing with a BMW?' he grinned.

His grin reminded me of the first time Julian the funeral director had seen me pull up in this car at the crematorium:

'There's nothing I'd like to see more in this world than your arse print on that bonnet after I've banged you senseless on it,' he'd said.

'We all have to treat ourselves once in a while, don't we?' I simpered at the constable now.

When we had shuffled over to the grass I said, 'Those three lovely old people in there are all recently bereaved.' OK, Di technically wasn't, as far as I knew, but she would be mourning the end of that bottle of Bristol Cream shortly. 'They have been through the ringer, bless them. All devastated for so long. And I have been trying to cheer them up. Show them a good time. Get them out of the house. So if you could find it in your heart to let us go just this once. I know they would blame themselves if I was charged with speeding and God only knows how that might set them back on their recovery. But you know what I will do? I will preach

139

about the dangers of speeding in my sermon this Sunday. I promise. Come along, if you like.'

The copper thought for a moment. He looked at the car from where Eric was looking up at the stars wistfully. Perhaps he saw his own father in Eric, or his grandmother in Di (God help him), or an old aunt in Linda. He looked back at my face, every muscle in it straining to stretch my features into those of an angel.

'Go on, then.'

Yes.

'Just this once, mind. If I catch you speeding again, I'll throw the bloody book at you, got it?'

I nodded gratefully and scampered back to my car.

'Shouldn't let women drive sports cars, let alone vicars,' he muttered to himself as he walked away.

Now *I* felt like throwing the book at *him*. The Bible. A large print version that would really do some damage. 'Not the time,' I told myself. 'Not the time.'

As I crawled away, keeping the gears low, Eric applauded and the girls cheered.

'Did you pull the clergy card?' Eric said, looking at me with sparkling eyes.

'I did,' I said, shame-faced.

'Well, I've pulled the doctor-in-an-emergency card before now, so don't be too hard on yourself.'

'I got my tits out for a policeman once,' Di said.

Linda shrieked and said, 'Was he going to arrest you?'

'No,' Di shrugged. 'But he did once I got my tits out.'

'You lot are going to have to sit through a sermon on road safety on Sunday,' I said. 'St Lawrence and his wonderful generosity to the poor will have to wait till next week.'

'I can't come on Sunday,' Linda said. 'I'm having my perm done.'

'Come on!' Eric said, 'The reverend is very entertaining. It won't be dull.'

'I bet, if this evening's anything to go by,' Linda sniggered.

As we drove on, I recalled Eric looking skyward as I'd lubed up the copper. There was something about the way he'd looked that reminded me of the way I felt when I prayed; when I felt heard by God. So I said 'Beautiful night' and glanced briefly up at the stars myself before returning my eyes to the road like a good driver.

'Yes,' he said. 'I was just thinking about that.'

'Oh?'

'Yes. You know, just after Beryl died I felt like I was standing on the tallest mountain. Mount Everest or something. Not that I've been there, but I've been up Snowdonia, so I can imagine. The wind is howling, screaming through you, and you try to scream too, but nothing is coming out. And then you look down and you can see the whole world going about its business as usual, as if nothing happened. I cursed life then, so many times, for bringing me grief. And yet I found myself holding grief in a certain degree of awe too.'

'Awe?' I asked.

'Yes. Because it's just like that,' he said, gesturing to the star-filled sky. 'It hushes everything inside you. Because it is so impossible to comprehend, so impossible to articulate.'

'I see,' I mused.

'My grief proved to me just how great my love for Beryl was. And I'm quite proud of how great that love was. Is.'

'You should be,' Linda said, leaning forward and patting him on the shoulder. She had no trouble hearing what he was saying now as I refused to go over thirty the whole way home.

TWENTY-EIGHT

The majority of rural parish congregations consist of older people. The few youngsters who come are dragged there by their elders, or come out of a sense of duty to them. However, most of those seniors in the flock are not driven to come to church out of any sense of spirituality. They come because that's what you do. That's what they have always done, since their elders dragged them there sixty years ago. Church is part of the weekly routine. For many, it's a social club, which is not a bad thing, especially for those who would feel alone otherwise. However, that sense of routine can very easily ossify and be resistant to any whiff of change, like – God forbid! – a young woman taking over as parish priest.

There was a church fundraiser for and at St Peter's, one of my churches. The usual tat and clothes that someone threw out for good reason would be on sale, as well as fairy cakes with so much Day-Glo icing my teeth ached just looking at them. Not my favourite event of the year by any stretch, but I had to show my face; a face which dropped when I entered the church and saw a tombola stand with ten bottles of booze lined up in front of it as prizes. These you might think have been the harmless accoutrements of the church fundraiser since Thomas à Becket was just a twinkle in his father's pants, but in my denomination, gambling and alcohol are forbidden on church premises (though thankfully not in the manse).

Good friends Marj and Sandra were in charge of the tombola, both in matching rollneck sweaters so thick they gave them both the look of whiplash sufferers.

'Um... sorry to be a spoil sport,' I said quietly, as members of the public milled about, 'but gambling and alcohol are forbidden on church premises.'

'You what?' said Sandra, looking me up and down. 'Who's gambling?'

I nodded at the revolving drum. 'The tombola. It's a form of gambling.'

'Well, it's hardly a high stakes poker table at Vegas, is it?' Sandra said derisively.

I thought, because she did have a bit of a point, and in the interest of peace, I should compromise here so I said, 'OK, I'm willing to overlook the tombola, but I'm afraid you can't have the alcohol.'

Sandra sized me up for a moment, then said, 'It's OK. I'll put it under the table out of sight.'

'No,' I said as she got busy secreting the bottles. 'Sorry. It needs to be off the premises.'

'Well, it's going to ruin the tombola if we do that. We've put all the numbers in there now, haven't we, Marj.'

Marj nodded. I don't remember her ever saying anything, but perhaps that's how their friendship worked – there wasn't room for her to talk as Sandra never seemed to come up for air.

'Can't you assign the ticket numbers on the booze to other prizes?' I offered.

'Where are we going to find ten new prizes at this time? Marj has put so much effort into this.'

Marjorie's eyes widened as Sandra pushed her into the firing line.

'We only sold so many tickets coz of the whiskey and wine,' Sandra went on, her face reddening and clashing awfully with her lilac pully.

'I'm really sorry, but you have to take the booze away.'

'Who says?' Sandra snapped.

'I do,' I said as patiently and quietly as I could. 'The church does. And I represent this church.'

'What do you know?' Sandra's voice was raised now. 'I'm not listening to you. You're the outsider here. We've done this for twenty years and not once has any other priest had a problem. And then you swan in here and ruin it for everybody.'

The punters were starting to be distracted from browsing the mildewed pages of second-hand books and getting high on sugary cakes. I didn't want to bring them down, so I walked away.

*

With some apprehension I went back to the same church the following Sunday to take the service, after which Derek cornered me. Derek was a local farmer. He was getting on and looked like Skeletor might if that archenemy of He-Man stopped going to the gym and decided to swap his hood, knee-length boots and thong for a tweed jacket, flat cap and wellies.

'Can I have a word?' he said.

'Of course,' I replied.

'Vestry?' he suggested.

I walked into the small office with him, then Derek closed the door behind us and stood in front of it barring my exit – I suppose the memo about how threatening that position could be had not yet reached him in the 1930s where he resided.

'You have no right to do what you did,' he began.

I had no doubt he was here on behalf of Marj and Sandra.

'You come to this church and you upset the applecart,' he crowed. 'That fair is the one event of the year where we can raise enough money to keep the church going for the rest of the year. You've upset Marj and Sandra. They refused to come today. And half the church will follow them before long. So you need to go and apologise. You were out of order. I don't know who you think you are, but—'

I couldn't believe how sanctimonious he was being. I'd seen him putting a paltry 20p in the collection plate every week before nipping down the pub for his four quid pints.

'I think,' I said firmly, 'no, I *know* I am an ordained priest, sent here by our polity to minister in this place, and I was simply upholding the constitutional practice and discipline of our church which clearly states alcohol is not permitted on any church premises.'

Derek's bony finger stabbed the air between us. 'I don't care what you think you were doing. You've broken this

144

church with your new-fangled nonsense. I should be taking this to your superiors.'

'I let the poxy tombola go ahead, Derek,' I said, shouting him down. 'And although the booze was eventually stashed in a car off the premises it was still handed out later as prizes, so yes, please do go to my superiors, but be sure the complaint is against me for allowing gambling and booze on church premises coz I therefore put this community at risk. Now, I'm going to leave, so if you could stand aside from the door.'

Coming from someone who often says balls to the rules and drinks like the fish that swallowed Jonah, you might think my stringency on this particular issue odd. But it is my job to make sure the church is a safe place, a place of sanctuary for anyone and everyone that needs it and that of course includes addicts, be it those addicted to gambling, alcohol or the myriad of addictions in between. Gary's terrible experience at theological college was never far from my mind and when I walked into that church fete and saw those bottles of booze lined up there, the grief in his eyes as he so abruptly left that communion broke my heart all over again. Who knows if there were other people among the punters at the fete who were in recovery too, or struggling in the midst of addiction? Walking in and seeing that whiskey and (very poor quality) wine lined up like that could have set them back years. I had to stand firm on this issue, perhaps more than any other. I'd even march Di out of St Augustine's whenever I heard bottles clinking in her shopping bags and make her stash them in a bush across the road until the service was over. She protested the first few times, but she soon got the message. I just couldn't risk something, like that which happened to Gary, happening to anyone in my church. I wasn't going to cower to Derek or Sandra, despite feeling totally shit about upsetting Sandra and totally shaken by being confronted by Derek in his bullish way.

So, I drove home with the radio turned up loud enough to drown out the swear words I was bellowing into the air and when I got home, since Spencer was away, to numb the pain and deal with the intense loneliness I felt in the clergy right then – Oh, irony of ironies – I cracked open a bottle of wine or two and got fuck-faced.

TWENTY-NINE

If you can't use alcohol for communion wine, what can you use?

Our rubric says we should use a 'drink based on the grape'. So it doesn't take Rick Stein to tell you the obvious accompaniment to your communion bread is therefore grape juice.

Liz, the steward at St John's (another of my six churches), took a sharp intake of breath like a car mechanic shortly before fleecing a customer, and said, 'I don't think we can use grape juice.'

'Why?' I asked.

Liz shifted about in her idiosyncratic way. She was a little resistant to new things, a little inflexible, but I'd thought at first that this was due only to her physical make-up. Liz, bless her, had only three toes on each foot. I knew this because she chose to wear open toed sandals every day, all year, whatever the weather. She would pass the collection plate round at the end of each service and then Liz would process down the aisle towards me on the podium from where I would be entranced by her waddling gait, which was very heavy-footed for someone who was missing a not insignificant percentage of each foot. When stewards arrived at the podium with the collection plate, they would invariably hand it up to me, but Liz always made me bend precariously down to her level to take the plate. She was short in stature and so I assumed her disinclination to hand the plate up was because her arms were too short and, what with her being a tridactyl, I had to fight with the image of Liz as a T-rex in an argyle sweater every time she lumbered towards me at collection time. But after a while, I began to think I had to teeter on the edge of the podium, bending like Mrs Overall to try to lift the plate steadily, which could barely contain the pile of twenty pence pieces the congregation had so generously given, because Liz was unwilling to change the habit of a lifetime. Perhaps the previous priests here had had names like Reverend Sneezy, Reverend Bashful or Reverend Doc. If so, Liz wasn't about to start lifting her arms a few more inches from her body and above her shoulders for some five-foot-eight giantess. And I assumed her aversion to grape juice might come from a similarly stubborn place.

'Well, it's expensive, is grape juice, and we only use a little bit in the service and it goes off, does grape juice, so I end up throwing the rest away. It's a waste.'

'Why don't you take the rest home and drink it?' I offered. 'No need to waste it.'

Liz thought for a moment before revealing the real nub of her opposition to grape juice. 'I don't like the taste.'

'Ah,' I said, resisting the urge to point out that communion wasn't exclusively for her.

'But I like cranberry juice,' she said brightly. 'I always have that. So I buy that for communion.'

'I don't think that quite fits with the Last Supper,' I said wryly, 'unless Jesus had a spot of cystitis that night, which considering the stress he was under I wouldn't be surprised if he did.'

Liz looked blank, so I elucidated.

'I think we need to find something else closer to wine, Liz.'

Liz waddled away grumbling – I'm not sure if it was this pesky young priest or her UTI that was irritating her.

At the next communion the following month I watched the eyes of each member of the congregation bulge as they took a sip of the 'blood of Christ, shed for you and for me'. We use little shot glasses for each person these days, as sipping from the same cup isn't considered hygienic any longer.

'Never did me no harm,' Liz said through her cold sores.

And when everyone had gone back to their seats, it was time for me to take a sip. Unlike the rest of the congregation kneeling at the table (joint replacements permitting) and facing the altar to take communion, I have to take it facing the congregation, all eyes on me.

My eyes also bulged as I drank and I wanted to spit it out, but I was afraid that whatever it was might irreparably soil the carpet and my reputation with the village. So I swallowed hard and smiled for my flock.

'Liz,' I said after the service. 'What did we drink at communion today?'

She sighed, 'Well, trying to find something that *everyone* likes and is based on the grape, my gosh, that's a full-time job, I can tell you.'

'Well, I really appreciate all your efforts,' I said through stained lips. 'So... what did you settle on in the end?'

'Vimto,' she sniffed with a hint of pride at her ingenuity. 'And I didn't dilute it so it looks more like wine.'

*

Communion bread should have been plain sailing after the wine debacle at St John's.

But no.

Every time I removed the cloth from the tray I would brace myself for whatever our Liz had provided us with this month. A full-on French style baguette was a nightmare. Flakes from the crust would fly everywhere as I broke it, some even ending up lodged in Loretta's cleavage or Trevor's toupee. Since more than half the congregation wore false teeth, the local dentist would be backed-up with appointments on Monday. And though they would chew and chew, when I came round again with the Vimto they'd still have a gob full of Jesus. So once again, I had to encourage Liz to find an alternative, something a little easier on the palette and one that I didn't have to maul in these hyper-hygienic times of ours.

The following month, I took a deep breath and whipped off the cloth to find bleached white sliced bread cut into little cubes and arranged neatly on the tray. Be careful what you wish for, I said to myself, as I tried desperately to symbolise the body of Christ broken on the cross with a soldier of Sunblest. But what concerned me more was the fact that the bread was soggy.

149

After the service I found Liz.

'Any idea why the bread was wet?' I sang, trying to hide my dread at what she might say.

'Oh,' Liz tutted, swiping the air with an untroubled limp wrist. 'I left it in my fridge last night to stay fresh, you know...'

'Ah,' I said, equally untroubled and heading for the vestry until she added:

'...and I was defrosting a chicken in there too.'

I stopped. Turned. And asked as casually as I could, 'And the chicken was where?'

'In the fridge,' Liz frowned.

'No, I mean, where exactly in the fridge?'

'Oh,' Liz smiled. 'Silly me. In the shelf above.'

'Above what?' I said, little beads of sweat beginning to form on my brow.

'Above the bread. So that's probably why the bread is wet, you know,' she said miming drops of raw chicken meltwater raining onto the body of Christ.

Somehow there wasn't an outbreak of salmonella in the parish that week. Not that everyone in the congregation took communion, which I found surprising when I first started in the job. I would often ask some of those who abstained why they didn't come forward. 'We're not cannibals like those Catholic lot,' I would say with a wink. 'We don't believe that the bread is actually Jesus's flesh as we eat it and the wine (or whatever gross undiluted squash we have) is his actual blood as we drink. We just use the bread and the wine to remember the story of the night before he was betrayed, when he sat with his disciples around a table and ate, broke bread and shared it with them, drank wine and asked them to remember the blood, his blood, that would be shed for them. You're just coming to that table and sharing in some of the love, that incredibly redemptive love.'

'No, no. I just don't do it,' they would usually answer. 'My parents never did it. So I don't do it either. It's the way it's always been.'

Change is a dirty word to many in the church.

*

Colin wasn't a fan of change either. He didn't come to church every week, and when he did he sat somewhere near the back, looking like a gargoyle descended from a rooftop that had found a faded pinstripe suit and a Barbour to wear.

I always went around the entire congregation before the service got underway to greet everyone and make them feel welcome. It didn't take a lot of my time at first given the size of the congregation, but the number of bums on seats had been rising nicely over the past couple of years.

When I reached Colin I said, 'Hiya. Nice to see you today.'

'How old are you?' he barked.

I was knocked off kilter slightly by this response, but recovered quickly with a giggly, 'You don't ask a lady how old she is,' trying to appeal to the chivalry of his age.

'Well, I want to know how old you are,' he demanded.

I cleared my throat and said with a wink, 'I'm old enough, let's put it like that.'

Colin leant forward and something creaked – his back or the pew or his self-esteem – as he jabbed a finger at me and spat, 'I feel so sorry for you. You've got nothing to offer these people here.'

'Really?' I said, feeling my face getting hot.

'You've got no life experience. You can't bring anything to this place. You don't understand what it means to have lived. You cannot relate to these people. You didn't even live through the Second World War. What can you teach these people about anything?'

'We're ready, Reverend,' I heard Erin say over my shoulder.

'Ah,' I said, pantomiming disappointment, 'so sorry, I have to go. But let me leave you with this. Jesus – remember him? – he'd changed the world before he died in his early thirties. Martin Luther King? Civil rights leader? Thirty-nine when he died.' But on second thoughts, I wasn't sure whether

Colin would be too impressed by the civil rights movement, so I added something colonial which I thought he might appreciate. 'Alexander the Great. Conquering countries from Greece to India and spreading the Hellenistic culture at just eighteen. Shakespeare wrote *Romeo and Juliet* in his mid-thirties. Mozart wrote his first symphony at eight. And of course you remember in Mark chapter ten, when parents tried to bring their children to Jesus for him to lay his hands on them and the disciples shooed them away. Jesus was not happy. He said to them, "Never stand between me and children because the kingdom of God belongs to such as these".'

Once in the pulpit I put aside the sermon I'd prepared with trembling hands and instead talked about 1 Corinthians Chapter 12, in which we are reminded that the human body has many parts but is nonetheless one.

'The eye cannot say to the hand *I don't need you*. And the head cannot say to the feet *I don't need you*. God has placed all the parts in the body, every one of them, just as he wanted them to be. Everyone, *everyone*,' I said pointedly in Colin's direction, 'has a part to play. Just as we are all baptised by one spirit so as to form one body. Jew or Gentile, black or white, woman or man, young or old.'

Colin sneered and stomped out of the church.

THIRTY

Jane and John weren't characters from a Ladybird book, they were real, they were engaged to be married and I was visiting them for a wedding prep meeting. In stark contrast to Candice and Ricky, Jane was a physio and John was an IT technician, they were in their early thirties and had a nice neat place in a nice neat village near St Augustine's.

As well as the questions I had put to Candice and Ricky – such as: Why get married? How will it change your relationship? What about kids and the financials? – I would usually ask the bride- and bridegroom-to-be:

'What are your expectations sexually after you're married?'

Jane and John blushed a little, as couples generally do at this point, but I ploughed on. It was important not to shy away from what could be a critical subject.

'Because I have to warn you, if you think you're going to get ten blowjobs a week, you'll be sorely disappointed.'

'Too right,' Candice had said to that.

'I fucking well will,' Ricky had replied.

Jane and John, however, were speechless and reddening further with every word I spoke.

So I quickly added, 'Don't worry. I'm not asking you to tell me now. Just write down your expectations on a piece of paper, both of you, then discuss it when you're alone.'

John and Jane looked at each other and began to twitter quietly, conferring about something for a while.

'Are you sure?'

'Yes, yes, we should do this. It's for the best.'

'Everything OK?' I asked. 'Please do not feel uncomfortable talking about sex. We all do it. We all think about it. And if we talked about it more with our partners and as a society as a whole, there'd be a whole lot more successful marriages. I talk about sex with my husband,' I said, leading by example. 'I even tell him about the fantasies I have. I have a thing for big hands, you see. Big strong hands, you know, the kind of hands farmers have. And there's plenty of them round these parts, isn't there? So when I preside over communion and I'm going down the line, everyone with their hands held out waiting for the bread, if I see a pair of those big thick grafters hands, well... I have to say, I come over all funny and I think to myself, I want those rugged hands caressing my body, all over. Oh, what those fingers could do to me! Rub my thigh with that hand right now before I give the salvation of Jesus Christ!'

Hashtag oversharing?

Jane was shaking her head so slightly and quickly I thought she might be shivering at first.

'No, no,' John said, snapping me out of my loin-quivering reverie. 'It's not that we don't want to talk about sex. It's that...' he took a deep breath and then went for it '...we've never had it.'

'Had what?' I said. Surely they didn't mean...

'Sex,' John clarified. 'We're both virgins.'

It seems Jane and John were indeed characters from a Ladybird book after all.

'It's not something we planned,' Jane added. We weren't saving ourselves or anything. We just both haven't ever had it and all our friends and family assume we have at our age, and we're too embarrassed to correct them now.'

'Oh–kay,' I said, trying not to add to their embarrassment.

'We don't even know what to do about contraception. I can't bring myself to talk about it to anyone for fear they'll ridicule me at my age,' Jane said.

'No, no, no,' I said firmly. 'No one's going to ridicule you.'

'Can you help us?' John said.

'Oh yes. As you might have guessed already, you've come to the right place,' I laughed.

John let out a laugh too. As did Jane. Relief rebounded around the room, like an inflated condom.

'No one's judging you here. And actually, if your marriage is based on a heretofore sexless relationship, then that says a lot about the love you have for each other. Having said that, sex is great,' I said with a grin. 'And I'm glad you're thinking about contraception,' I smiled, recalling Ricky's mum's house infested with kids and dogs and wincing at the irony that it was the sweet, sensitive Janes and Johns of this world that were always wise enough to use contraception when it was more of their kind that we actually needed, if any, on this overpopulated rock of ours. 'Jane, you can go to a nurse at the practice and speak very confidentially and honestly about your needs. They talk about contraception with patients all day long. It's not a big deal to them, so you've nothing to be ashamed of. I often talk to the nurses when I'm considering changing to a new method. You'll find what's right for you. They'll go through all the options. There are many these days. Although I wouldn't necessarily recommend having a coil fitted first of all,' I said, clenching.

THIRTY-ONE

My homily on the horny fresh in my mind, I arrived at the church's national synod. A bit like the church retreats, but always in a far more exotic location – like Coventry – and with hundreds more priests from far and wide so that the venue stank of Old Spice and mothballs.

The big talking point of this year's meeting was the proposal of a code of conduct which the church was expecting all of us to sign up to. We don't have contracts in our church. How could you possibly contract someone to do God's work? So we have a covenant, an understanding. Similarly, we are not paid a salary, we are given a stipend, just enough so we don't have to seek employment elsewhere and we can concentrate on doing the work of the church. But these days we live in the world of GDPR, safeguarding and compliance, and although I'd rather be waterboarded than fill out another tedious risk assessment, we do need something to protect us from, for example, working ninety-hour weeks, and something to encourage those who'll use health and safety as an excuse to do fuck all to work more than fifteen hours a week.

So the code of conduct was a contract in disguise. But apart from the more mundane issues of working hours and pay there was a litany (and not in the warm and fuzzy liturgical sense) of draconian dos and don'ts, which would penetrate the private lives of all us clergy. The one which stood out to me was paragraph 79a, which said:

If you are looking at pornographic material, you must inform your supervisor. If you are experiencing any marital difficulties, you must inform your supervisor. If you are experiencing sexual feelings for anyone in your congregation who is not your spouse you must inform your supervisor.

Hadrian was at the synod. It was so nice to see someone with dress sense.

'Saw you creeping out of a room that was not yours this morning,' I whispered as a speaker took the podium to introduce the code of conduct.

Hadrian blushed and grinned. 'You spying on me?'

'No. I was getting up early to go down to the gym.'

'Ah. Well, yes,' he whispered. 'Walk of shame. But the best thing about these things is the hotel fun.'

'How was it?' I asked.

'Eye-watering,' Hadrian giggled.

'I want all the details later,' I said, getting up.

'Are you going to speak?' he whispered, nodding at the podium.

'Absolutely. Have you read this shit?' I said.

'I tried,' he said, 'but *Strictly* was on.'

I nodded in sympathy. 'Well, someone has to say something. It reads like Leviticus.'

'Oh, but that's my favourite.' Hadrian clapped his hands quietly together like a child before a birthday cake. 'Especially verse twenty-two, you know, the part that says *Do not have sexual relations with a man as one does with a woman, that is abomination.*'

'You should get up as well,' I said.

'No, no, I'm going to keep my head down, thank you very much. Perhaps you should too.'

'Um...,' I said, pantomime pondering, 'I'm going to keep my head up. High. Wish me luck!'

'Oh, you'll be fine. It's the church that needs luck,' he said with a wink.

I went over to the side of the podium where empty seats awaited those who wanted to speak on any agenda item as it was being introduced on stage. As I sat waiting, I started to wonder if Hadrian was right, if I was doing the right thing by speaking out on this issue, or just asking for trouble. But then I got the nod from the chair and it was too late to back out.

I took to the podium grinning benignly at the room. I spotted Uncle Peter and he gave me the kind of look your mum might have as you walked on stage with her tea towel on your head in the school nativity. Then I spotted Oliver Roach looking up at me from beneath eyebrows as spiky as sea urchins and I felt my knees wobble ever so slightly.

Oliver was, technically, my boss and in many ways he reminded me of David Tanner, the principal of my theological college in Cambridge. They both had the social skills of Twitter, they were both excruciating to chat to and they both looked down on me, which was some feat as they were both considerably shorter than the five glamourous feet and eight gorgeous inches of me. But sometimes – *sometimes* – I don't think they even knew they were doing so.

The thing with the patriarchy is that it gives many men the power to fuck women over without them even knowing they are doing it. I don't believe all men get up in the morning thinking 'I'm going to screw over all the women I encounter today'. In a way, they are victims of the system too because of the chauvinistic values it imbues them with, but the consequences for them are not so devastating as they can be for the women they steamroller over with those values. In the same way, many white people, no matter how non-racist they think they are, cannot know what it is to be the only black person in the room trying to get their voice heard.

A day-long session of a committee, which I sat on with fourteen other priests, headed by Oliver, was once coming to an end and I noticed that Kingsley was the only person who hadn't said a word for the entire meeting. Kingsley was also the only black person on the panel. I hoped I wouldn't embarrass him with what I was about to say, but I felt he would probably appreciate it more from me, the only other BAME person on the panel – yes, didn't I mention that? BAME *and* female. Sweet baby Jesus, if I had been disabled too, I would have been the triple threat.

'Oliver,' I said before he could wrap things up. 'I was just aware that Kingsley hasn't spoken all day and I really value his ministry so I for one would be really interested to hear what he has to say on the subjects we've been discussing.'

Some of the other priests started nodding like dashboard dogs as the car pulls away.

Oliver looked as if he'd just been sick in his mouth as Kingsley said in my direction, 'Thanks so much for giving me the opportunity to speak. I have been really keen to speak all day, so...' and off he went endowing the group with something beautiful and useful which we wouldn't have heard if it was up to Oliver, because Kingsley is not as bolshy as me. His voice would not have been heard, not because he should have spoken up, but because Oliver didn't even notice he hadn't.

Back on the podium at the synod, as I opened my mouth to speak, I noticed Oliver still had that nauseated look about him. And I think it was me that was the cause. But instead of baulking at this, I told myself that this was exactly why I should be speaking right now and it loosened up my tongue, perhaps a little too much, in hindsight.

'Mr President, members of the synod,' I began. 'I have many questions about the code of conduct, particularly paragraph 79a.'

There was a murmur from the delegates. I thought I heard 'She would' from one old fart.

'My supervisor is a lovely man,' I said smiling warmly in Uncle Peter's direction, 'but I know that he would feel a lot more uncomfortable than me if I told him I was masturbating about the organist or if I told him that in my spare time when I'm on Pornhub I search out Brazilian plumber services ebony housewife. Also paragraph 79a seems to exclude open relationships or throuples, where experiencing sexual feelings and indeed acting on them with someone who is not your spouse is completely acceptable.'

I looked at Hadrian and recalled that time in college when we made a pact:

'When we get out in the real world and minister for real,' I said, 'we have to be real too, not Biblical anachronisms like these relics that run this place would have us be.'

And it spurred me on. 'This part of the proposed code is therefore not only discriminatory, but deeply unrealistic. May I refer you to the wonderful erotica of the unwedded couple in that Old Testament book, The Song of Songs. Members of the synod, I cannot support this proposal. Thank you very much.'

'Hear hear!' cried Hadrian.

Then a few others joined him – the vocal version of nodding dogs.

As I left the podium, I glanced at Oliver. His face was hot and sweaty, with anger I think, in hindsight, though I could just imagine the same look on his face when, as a student, he no doubt tented his Bible across his lust-turgid lap after taking another ravenous peek at The Song of Songs.

THIRTY-TWO

Spencer was turning fifty. That's a big one. Half a century on the planet. With the multitude of ways in which our number could be up, it is a miracle to hang on for more than a few decades – even Jesus didn't manage that – so I wanted to celebrate Spencer's milestone by organising a huge surprise party for him. When he was based in Edinburgh in the years before we met, he not only squeezed every drop of juice out of the pilot's lifestyle – girl in every port kind of stuff – but he augmented that by playing guitar in a band with his two mates, Shez on bass and Trey on drums. Sex, Rock 'n' Roll and no doubt a few intoxicants along the way too – but that's a whole other book, which I'll leave him to pen.

Shez and Trey still lived in Edinburgh and, like most budding rock stars the world over, soon got married, had kids and realised they had to get a proper job when neither Clive Davis nor even the last resort of Simon Cowell came knocking down their door wielding a recording contract with loads of noughts on it. But, like Spencer, they had done pretty well for themselves without a Svengali in their lives. In fact Shez and his wife Rita loved nothing more than to hold sensational parties in their souped-up home, which even had a special black-lit *room* (not a lowly garage) for their Lamborghini Spyder. The car made my BMW look like a Lada; their house made my manse look like somewhere in which you might give birth to a messiah, and in it they were keen to host Spencer's fiftieth and add it to their back catalogue of legendary shindigs.

In secret we invited all of Spencer's friends and I would get him up to Edinburgh on the pretext of going to stay with Shez and Rita for the weekend because I had to have a church meeting with Oliver Roach, who was based there. I didn't have a meeting with him at all, but I asked my boss to go along with the ruse so that I could get Spencer to drive me to his office while Shez and Rita set up the party and all the guests piled into their house.

'Thanks for letting me hide out here,' I said to Oliver, peeking out of the window to see if Spencer was still waiting in the car. 'Are you sure you don't want to come to the party?'

Oliver stuttered as he tried to be consistent in his responses to my repeated invitation: 'Oh no, no, unfortunately I can't. I have to have that... um... other thing and then an early start in the morning, so...' he smiled weakly.

'Martin is going,' I said, hoping that the knowledge of his opposite number in the neighbouring district attending would make him feel more comfortable. 'Uncle Peter, Keith too. You know Keith – purveyor of the finest cream horns – and the odd cake too,' I laughed awkwardly at my seaside humour which I thought, for some misguided reason, Oliver would share.

'Ah. Well, it would be nice to see them all, but please pass on my apologies. And have a good time,' he said which translated as 'Fuck off now please'.

So I did.

Spencer drove us back to Shez and Rita's where he was delighted to see all his friends bursting with well-wishes and all the fridges bursting with booze. The buffet, I and my ministerial mates noted, was far from the beige ones of church dos. Shez and Rita made sure it was baked Camembert topped with cranberries and Cointreau rather than cheese and pineapple hedgehogs, Belgian chocolate fountains rather than Rice Krispies cakes. We partied as hard that Friday night as such an occasion deserved and in the morning I woke with a hangover which lasted until Sunday and made me feel as if God was punishing me, for that Sunday was Palm Sunday, the first day of Holy Week, a priest's busiest time of year next to Christmas.

Palm Sunday is the day we commemorate Christ's triumphant arrival in Jerusalem on the back of a donkey, greeted by the people with cheers and hosannas. How their tune would change a few days later as Jesus hung on the cross and was rejected and mocked by these same people.

That week, I would have to pack in a whopping twenty-one services, what with Maundy Thursday, Good Friday and Easter Sunday too. But after the final service, in which we celebrate Christ's resurrection, a symbol of the possibility of rebirth in our own lives, a day in which we mark the end of the Lenten season of penitence and fasting by stuffing ourselves full of chocolate eggs in a kind of religious bulimia, I was looking forward to jetting off with Spencer to Kenya for a bit of rejuvenation of my own under the African sun where my cousin was getting married.

On Monday morning, we were taking our suitcases out to the car when the landline rang.

'Leave it,' Spencer tutted.

I was inclined to agree. If it was urgent they could call my mobile. So I carried on packing the car. But the phone carried on ringing.

I huffed. Like a moth to a flame, I couldn't resist finding out who it was.

'Hello?'

'Hello, it's Oliver.'

'Oh, hi, Oliver,' I chirped in surprise. 'How are you?'

'I'm OK, thank you.'

It was so rare that Oliver called, that I joked, 'Uh-oh. No matter who said I did it, I wasn't there, I didn't do it and I've got a great alibi.' I laughed.

Oliver didn't even attempt a chuckle. 'Well, actually, this is not the time to be joking.'

'Everything all right?'

'No, I'm afraid not. Someone has actually put in a formal complaint about you.'

I sat down, my heart pounding, my mouth like Jesus's flip-flop. What the fuck! What...? Who have I upset? I couldn't imagine. Derek and Sandra, yes, but that was all done and dusted. Well, actually it needed a good going over with some Mr Sheen but there was at least a kind of sulky détente between us these days.

'What complaint? About what?' I stuttered.

'It was about the party in Edinburgh and your behaviour there.'

'Spencer's birthday party?' I said, incredulous. 'Why would anyone complain about me there? It was a private party, invite only, in a private house, just with friends of ours.'

'There's a certain photo – I'm sure you know which one I refer to – that has upset a few of your guests. I need you to give me a formal response to the complaint by three o'clock this Sunday, OK? Thank you,' he said and hung up.

'What's wrong?' Spencer said coming from the driveway and seeing me trembling.

'Someone's made a complaint about me at your party.'

'For doing what?' he asked quite legitimately.

I snapped, 'I don't fucking know. Some photo. I haven't got a clue what's going on. I know as much as you.'

'It's OK,' he said, giving me a much-needed hug as I started to have flashbacks of the time in college when David told me of a complaint against me then left me to stew on what that complaint could possibly be for the entire Christmas vacation because he was too sexually repressed to talk about breasts.

'I can't go through this again. I won't go through this again,' I said, picking up the phone and calling Oliver back.

Meanwhile Spencer started scrolling through the photos on his phone to see if there was anything incriminating from the party. As I waited for Oliver to pick up, Spencer showed me a photo of him holding a bottle of lager as if it was his cock and me going down on the bottle.

I grimaced. Not my finest hour, but who at the party would have had a problem with that?

'Hello?' Oliver said.

'Oliver, I need to know exactly what this complaint is about.'

'You should know,' he said in a terrifying echo of David Tanner during Breast-gate.

'Oh my goodness, Oliver, why can't you just say? I believe the bloody code of conduct compels you to show me the complaint form.'

Oliver babbled for a moment then said, 'Very well, I'll forward the complaint form to you now. But you mustn't discuss it with anyone. It is highly confidential.'

'OK. Thank you,' I gasped and ran to my laptop.

After a few hour-long minutes, the form appeared in my inbox. A few stabs at my mouse and the complaint form was revealed, but I didn't recognise the name of the complainant.

'Who is it?' Spencer asked.

'Fran Curtis,' I shrugged. 'Pretty sure there was no one called Fran at the party.' I read on:

My daughter and her husband attended a private birthday party in Edinburgh on Friday. They were shocked to see the behaviour of the Reverend Laura Chapman at the party. I showed Rev Roach a photo of Rev Chapman in an intimate embrace with a man whom someone described as a 'bishop' kissing her. I have since heard his name is Martin Gough. Laura Chapman's pose in this picture was deeply inappropriate at best, disgusting at worst, which revealed her underwear and buttocks. What if it gets on Facebook?

As I read the email, Spencer scrolled through more photos and found one of myself and Martin Gough in the kitchen, arms around each other, my left leg hitched up around him in my standard party photo pose – well, when you wear hold-ups, as I like to, you want to show them off. Martin had grabbed my leg and hitched it up just that little bit further as the shutter clicked revealing the edge of the fantastically lacey knickers I had bought for the occasion and a sliver of buttock. Just a sliver. There was, frankly, more meat visible on the vegan bruschetta on the work surface behind me.

I got straight on the phone to Martin.

'Hello?'

'Martin, have you heard about this complaint against us?'

'No. What complaint?'

'About that photo of me and you at the party.'

Martin cackled.

'What?' I said.

'Really?' he laughed. 'That's hilarious.'

'In what way is that hilarious?' I scowled down the phone.

It soon became clear that, for Martin, it *could* be hilarious, because no one had made a complaint against him, just me – despite the fact that it takes two to Argentine tango, as we appeared to be doing in the photo.

'I could lose my job over this, Martin,' I said tearfully.

'That's ridiculous. It's just a photo at a party. Don't worry,' he said, still giggling. 'Just meet it head on. They haven't got a leg to stand on, pardon the pun!' And he burst out laughing again.

'Martin!' I scolded.

'Sorry. Sorry,' he said, coughing the amusement out of his throat. 'Look, why did this happen?'

'I don't know. And since I've been forbidden to talk about it with anyone, I can't really investigate.'

'Well, I haven't been forbidden to talk about it with anyone,' Spencer said boldly over my shoulder.

I hung up on feckless Martin and looked at Spencer, who looked queasy.

'I've just realised who Fran Curtis is.'

'Who?' I said.

'Rita's mum.'

'Rita? As in Shez and Rita? Your best friends?'

Spencer nodded.

'It says here that they were *shocked to see my behaviour.* That doesn't sound like them.'

The week of sermons I'd just given crowded into my head. Sermons in which I'd described how the people of Jerusalem went from partying and celebrating Jesus's arrival to hanging him out to dry. Such destructive U-turns in attitude really can happen, it seemed.

Spencer was as baffled as I was, so he got on the phone straight away to Shez.

'Me and Rita?' Shez cried down the phone. 'Shocked?' He laughed, 'Blimey, Spence, it would take a bit more than that to shock us. Remember that time backstage in London when Trey did a shit in a pint glass and that groupie ate it? I have to admit to a smidgen of distaste at that. But your lovely wife showing a bit of thigh, even if she was the Pope, does not come anywhere close to my top ten most shocking moments.'

And it wasn't long before he discovered that Rita had shown her mother, Fran, pictures of the party. Rita had innocently told her mum about how much fun I was *for a vicar person*. The trouble was, Fran happened to be a regular at church where Oliver preached and she'd mentioned with her tongue firmly lodged in her cheek about the party her daughter had hosted last week where one of Oliver's priests had let it all hang out.

'Looks like it was getting a bit racy,' she'd said with a wink.

To which Oliver had said, 'Would you like to make a complaint?'

'Oh,' Fran said, taken aback. 'I don't think that's necessary.'

But apparently Oliver did. He prised a bit more information out of Fran and then told her not to worry, he would deal with it. He must have filled out the complaint form on her behalf. Then, having received the complaint form, from himself, Oliver fulfilled his duty by initiating a complaints procedure with such unusual degrees of alacrity and zeal one can only assume this was something he had been hoping for for some time. Since the committee meeting perhaps? Or since my speech at the synod?

I knew just how Janet Jackson must have felt when Justin Timberlake got her tit out at the Super Bowl halftime show. Of course, it was planned, choreographed slickly by Jackson and Timberlake, like everything else they've ever done, but after half a million complaints and a half a million dollar fine to the network, someone had to be the scapegoat. Was it Justin? No, it was Janet. Was it the man? No, it was the woman. Networks and radio stations blacklisted her music, not his. Her career took a hit, his stardom only grew. Timberlake performed and took home two trophies at the subsequent Grammy awards; Jackson's performance at the same event was scrapped. It took squeaky clean Justin thirteen years to admit that he 'benefited from a system that condones misogyny and racism'.

I was not on stage in front of millions of people. I was at a friend's house, wearing – as is my right as a human being – whatever the fuck I wanted to wear, and doing – without hurting others – whatever the fuck I wanted to do. As was Martin. But when it came to the crunch we were judged differently because of our genders and because of his position of power. I was Janeted. He was Justined.

But I wasn't going to roll over and take my punishment like a good little girl, not this time. Rita had a word with her mum, who was devastated to know just how dramatically things had escalated since her comment to Oliver in church. She asked Oliver that any complaint be dropped and a few days later, in the middle of my holiday, half of which had been ruined by the stress of not knowing what was happening, I received this terse email.

...the complainant indicates that she wishes to withdraw the complaint.

From a formal point of view, the complaint is now withdrawn. This matter is now at an end.

'No, no, no, Oliver, this matter is not at an end. You're not getting off that lightly,' I thought.

The following weekend, we both attended another synod, and as soon as I saw him through the crowded conference hall I headed over to arrange a time for a Thigh-gate debriefing. The moment he caught sight of me he seemed to develop a terrible bladder infection that meant he had to keep nipping off to the toilet whenever I approached him that day, but in the evening as the council dispersed, I cornered him between the coffee urn and the flapjacks.

'I must just nip to the—'

'Don't worry, Oliver. This won't take long. Then you can go to the little boys' room,' I said with the emphasis on little.

He looked around the room as if for help. None came.

'The complaint,' I began.

'Oh, yes,' he said, smoothing his combover down over his forehead where, on Ash Wednesday, he would have left the sooty smudge of the cross unwiped as he walked through town after leaving the church service, signalling his piety to all.

'I was just wondering if you'd given any thought to why Martin wasn't dragged through this debacle, as I was.'

'Excuse me?'

'Martin was in the photo too. Martin was touching me, kissing me. As a senior leader in the church, do you not think he would have to take some responsibility for this, if I did? Do you not see that there is an imbalance here? One which, if you overlook, constitutes an abuse of privilege?'

'Abuse?' he reddened.

'I forgive you,' I said. 'It can't be easy.'

'What?' he scowled.

'Being a white middle-aged man in authority, I understand that you really struggle to see inequality.'

'Look—'

'It must have been so hard for you to see how discriminatory it was that only I was the subject of that complaint and not both Martin and I.'

169

I strutted off as Oliver started babbling incoherently. He would make a perfect prime minister.

THIRTY-THREE

I conduct burials. I conduct cremations. And sometimes I conduct the burial of cremated ashes.

Today Julian and I were burying the ashes of Tom in the presence of his close family: his widow Nancy, their three kids and their spouses. Well, two of their spouses. The third, Ben, had had an argument with his wife, Tom's youngest daughter, about the burial. He reckoned it was a 'bloody waste of time and stress'. They'd already had a cremation, he said, which he'd had to lose a day's work for. Now they wanted to have a burial too? 'A bit greedy, isn't it?' Ben probably expected that Tom's urn would be, as urns are for many people, a nice bookend on the mantelpiece, or that the ashes would be scattered at Tom's favourite beach in Bournemouth, hopefully not during an onshore wind that left holidaymakers with a fine dusting of the dead stuck to their sun-lotion-smeared bodies.

I could see Ben's point. There's something a bit having your cake and eating it about a burial of ashes. I mean, why not just bury the body if you're still going to bury the ashes? Neither burial nor cremation are exactly eco-friendly, so burying the ashes is like sticking *two* fingers up at Greta Thunberg. So I imagine Donald Trump will opt for a burial of his ashes. In a golden cock-shaped urn.

As Julian and I drove into the cemetery I was telling him all about Thigh-gate.

'Oliver has it in for me, I explained. 'He'd love to see the back of me.'

'I'd love to see the back of you too,' Julian grinned, 'as I took you up the bum.'

I rolled my eyes and smiled at Tom's family who were waiting in the car park.

'Bollocks,' whispered Julian as we parked.

'What?' I whispered back.

'I forgot to keep some ashes spare for the family to take. They told me how much they wanted some.'

I could just hear Ben now: 'They want to cremate him, bury the ashes, *and* keep some? Are we going to have to do that bloody trip to Bournemouth after all with a sandwich bag full of your father?'

'So?' I said to Julian.

'I don't think I can get the casket open now. Not without a screwdriver.'

For a burial of ashes the remains are housed in a casket, which looks a bit like a coffin for a young hobbit, sealed by a screw on each corner.

'What about a penknife?' I asked, pulling one out from under my cassock.

Julian's eyes widened. 'What do you carry that around for?' he squawked.

'To cut the balls off any randy funeral directors,' I winked.

He grabbed it and I brought the little casket surreptitiously from the back seat. Obscuring him from the family's view with my back, Julian went about undoing the lid, passing each of the little screws he liberated to me before prising the box open. To Tom's family, who were by now getting antsy, we must have looked like a couple of boy-racers shiftily doing lines of coke in a layby.

'Done it,' he said triumphantly, before screwing up his nose. 'Pooh!'

'What?'

'It still stinks in there.'

I looked askance at Julian, so he explained.

'Tom was a farmer, so they wanted him cremated with things he'd produced. The coffin was stuffed with leeks, carrots, potatoes, you name it. When we put the burners on, the crematorium smelt like cabbage soup.'

'Eeuw. But what can we put the ashes in?' I asked.

'Balls,' Julian grumbled.

We looked around the car. I looked over my shoulder. Tom's family were eyeing us suspiciously now. I opened the glovebox.

'What's this?' I said pulling out some Tupperware.

'My lunch,' Julian said.

'Not any more,' I said, emptying his cheese and pickle sandwiches and replacing them with a healthy portion of the ashes.

With part of Tom safely in Julian's lunchbox, I passed each screw back to Julian.

'My dream come true,' he grinned as he took the last one. 'Always wanted a screw from you.'

'Piss off,' I said.

'Especially since the hot pants,' he said, his eyes glazing over as he reminisced about the funeral of Lou.

*

Michelle was Lou's granddaughter and she was making all the funeral arrangements. She had obviously been very close to Lou and enjoyed showing me photos of her when I went round for the funeral visit. Lou was a vision with her blue rinse hair, cyan eyeshadow and bright red lipstick adorning her toothless mouth, which looked like the opening of a drawstring bag. She always wore square-heeled slingbacks which her swollen ankles bulged over like bread rising in an oven, Nora Batty tights and a pinny over her blouse to keep it clean while she did the housework.

'She loved leopard print,' Michelle smiled, pointing out the blouse underneath the apron. 'So we're all going to wear something leopard print to the funeral. And we were wondering if you could too.'

My eyes lit up briefly until I realised, 'I don't have anything leopard print,' I sighed. 'Except...'

Michelle was on the edge of her seat. 'Yeah?'

'The hot pants I use for pole dancing.'

Michelle's jaw hit the floor. 'You're a pole dancer?'

'I do pole fitness, yeah,' I smiled.

'Amazing,' she said. 'Please, please, will you wear them to the funeral? Lou would love it. I would love it. Please,' she sang.

'Well,' I said enjoying the sparkle in Michelle's eyes, 'I have to wear the whole cassock thing unfortunately.'

Michelle wilted.

So I added, 'But how about I wear them underneath, so you will know and Lou will know that I'm joining the leopard print party?'

Michelle was over the moon.

On the day, the cortege looked like a Rod Stewart convention being crashed by the Bet Lynch fan club. I felt like a right party pooper in my black gown, so I collared Michelle before the procession to the church began.

'Michelle! Michelle! Come here!'

I led her behind the horse and carriage that would deliver Lou in all the East End splendour she deserved, and hoisted up my cassock revealing I had absolutely nothing on underneath save my hot pants.

Michelle yelped and clapped her hands together. 'That is awesome,' she cried.

And then it was time to process, Julian and I in front of the carriage, the family behind. It was October and the weather was turning. I should have known what would happen – even Michael Fish could have predicted the gusts that ensued, whipping my cassock up like Marilyn's dress over a subway air vent, showing my hot pants off to mourners and passers-by alike.

If Oliver Roach could see me now.

'Are you trying to give me the horn?' Julian whispered, drool running down his chin.

'Spoiler alert, Julian, darling,' I said. 'Women don't dress for male consumption.'

THIRTY-FOUR

The communities in which I preached for the first years of my priesthood were so small, only a few thousand strong, that everyone would turn out for the switching on of the Christmas lights. It would be the most excitement many of them had had since Sandra had chased her husband down Privet Street with a wooden spoon in February. I, however, would rather have been at home watching *Love Island* – I know, I'm going to hell.

Before the actual flicking of the switch there would be carols sung by kids from the local schools. I would have to stand there with a fellow priest on the scaffolding stage, freezing my tits off, smiling inanely as if the little tykes' tuneless droning was in fact the heavenly host. Then it fell to us to do a little speech about the meaning of Christmas to a few thousand people who looked at us as if we were aliens since they thought the real meaning of Christmas was getting themselves in debt buying enough food to feed a small developing country, enough toys to stock Hamleys so their kids didn't feel left out among all their Nike-wearing, VR-playing friends, and sitting round a table creaking under the weight of wine bottles and a giant overcooked turkey with family they wished they'd never invited.

Father Wayne was a Catholic priest who shared the stage with me that year in a show of ecumenical unity. He desperately wanted to be the one who addressed the crowd with a religious message, something which I was more than happy to let him do. I owed him one anyway, since a couple had approached me after Sunday service asking me to expel the bad juju they felt in their new home. Exorcisms were not my bag, but I said I'd be happy to bless their house if it would help. They said it would, so I hightailed it over to Father Wayne's church as I knew he would have holy water to spare. He showed me into the vestry where I expected to find the blessed H_2O in the beautiful silver chalice of Catholic services, but instead saw shelf upon shelf groaning under the weight of dozens of plastic four-litre milk bottles, a label sellotaped over each Tesco one with HOLY WATER printed on it in Comic Sans. Armed with a liturgy from Father Wayne and a generous helping from one of the milk jugs, I went to the haunted house and had the family splashing water all over it as if they were at Centre Parcs. The house had a faint odour of cow juice when I left and would possibly have issues with rising damp in the future, but the family were happy and felt their home was safe – that's all that mattered.

So when it came to the Christmas lights, Father Wayne and I agreed that I would act like his MC.

'Good evening, Little Buntingsfield, are you having a good time?' I screeched down the mic.

The crowd murmured back as if they were made up entirely of teenagers who'd been asked if they wanted a sandwich while gaming. So I decided to miss out the next bit I'd planned which I had dreamt might go something like this:

ME: When I shout Jesus, you shout Christ! Jesus.'

CROWD: Christ.

ME: Jesus.

CROWD: Christ.

Instead, I handed over to Wayne who proceeded with a pious lecture that soon had the audience losing the will to live.

I was daydreaming about hot mince pies and custard when a producer from the local radio station covering the event whispered to me, 'Wrap it up! You've got twenty seconds until the lights go on.'

'OK, OK,' I hissed back. 'Thank you, Father Wayne,' I said, gently wrestling the mic from him even though he was in mid-sentence, something about how the wise men coming from the East tells us how the perceived wisdom of the Orient must turn West to be saved – bell-end. 'Such… um… stirring words.' I was still thinking about custard. 'So a quick final prayer from me to you and from all the churches in our lovely community…' But the producer had flustered me. My mind went blank. A prayer. *A prayer.* Every prayer I'd ever thought of had gone from my brain. I could feel those twenty seconds ticking away, the pressure was overwhelming. *Say something!* So I opened my mouth and said, 'May God bless you and everyone you love this Christmas and... um... and those that you're not very fond of too.'

Father Wayne looked at me askance, but whatever I had babbled seemed to resonate with the crowd, jittery about their imminent family gatherings. They cheered and applauded, then engaged with the countdown with unprecedented gusto, Sandra's pursuit of her trouserless husband a distant memory.

*

Crowd-pleasing is part of a priest's job at Christmas. For many people, it is the only time of year when they attend church, looking to be entertained by the cuddly story of a new-born baby surrounded by little lambs and a donkey to brighten up the miserable winter. For us clergy, it is an even busier time than Easter, and I have to do more carol concerts than there are chocolates in your advent calendar.

Some people are, I'm afraid, disappointed when they come to my church in December seeking pretty nativity stories. Because the nativity story is not a pretty one. In fact it is awful. It is the story of a dysfunctional family, of two youths who aren't married, but the girl has got herself knocked up. They are living under occupation and are made to travel miles to register themselves so that the occupying forces can keep tabs on them. After a long and uncomfortable journey, the girl's baby is born in less than sanitary conditions. Then, when the King hears the prophecy that a new Jewish king has just been born, he has all Jewish boys under the age of two killed. Christmas is about genocide as much as it is about mistletoe and wine.

'But it's all about the kids,' people say. 'Christmas is for the kids. It's about Santa and reindeer.'

My response? 'Yes, we should think about children at this time of year. Let's think about all the children around the world who are enslaved or made to be child soldiers. There are at least fourteen countries in the world where children are forced into combat,' I said during one Christmas service to a congregation with *When are we singing 'Good King Wenceslas'?* written all over their faces. 'On the communion table,' I went on, 'there are fourteen envelopes by fourteen candles. Inside each envelope are two cards, both identical, with the name of one of each of those fourteen countries written on them. I would like anyone who wishes to, to approach the table, light a candle, put one of those two cards next to the candle and take the other home and keep it visible, so that on Christmas Day when you're knee deep in wrapping paper, you can see that card and if it says, for example, *Congo*, you will hopefully take a moment to pray for the child soldiers in Congo.'

Some members of the congregation did just that and then we launched into the carol they were thirsty for.

There were sniggers from the younger members of the congregation during the carol. I assumed it was, as usual, because we had got to the line *heat was in the very sod that the saint had printed*. But I noticed all eyes were now on the communion table. I turned to see Colombia was aflame. I had overlooked some fire safety precautions that would have been second nature to a child soldier in Yemen well versed in the art of explosives.

THIRTY-FIVE

I am not a total Scrooge when it comes to kids at Christmas. Against my better judgement I even invite them to bring in the presents they got on Christmas Day. During the service they each get up to show off their new favourite toy and I stand there like Larry Grayson on *The Generation Game* saying, 'Didn't he do well?'

'What about you, Alfie?' I beamed. 'Do you want to show us what you got?'

Alfie's parents nudged him into the aisle and as he steadied himself on the back of the pew I realised he was already wearing his present – a pair of *Ben 10* roller skates.

'Oh wow,' I said trying to find a fuck to give – well, it was the season of good will. 'Why don't you show us how good you are on them? Have a go up the aisle!' I said, though my mind was screaming, *No, no! Why would you say that? Alfie's an accident waiting to happen when he's not on wheels.*

Alfie wasn't sure, but Alfie's dad prised his fingers from the back of the pew and shoved him towards me. Alfie flew across the flagstones and nearly took out Di, who was tottering back towards the organ after popping out for a wee – or for a shot of her gin, which I made her keep in the bush over the road, despite her protestations that she would make sure no alcoholics got hold of it. Alfie zoomed towards me and I side-stepped out of the way leaving Alfie to slam his wheels into the podium and faceplant inches from the communion table.

'Well done,' I said, encouraging the bemused congregation to applaud, 'You'll be professional in no time. Keep practising!' I said as I picked him up and sent him rolling back to his pew. 'Now,' I said, looking around the room. 'Who else wants to show their lovely present?'

A hand shot up in the air – the kind that is on the end of the annoying swot in class who answers every question the teacher poses.

'Sarah?' I smiled like a circus clown. 'Yes, come and show us what you got!'

Sarah's parents jiggled with excitement as Sarah bounded towards me with some kind of remote-control helicopter.

'And what's this?' I asked.

'A drone,' Sarah said, politely stopping herself from adding, '*Of course.*'

'Do you want to—?'

She didn't need my permission. She twiddled a few knobs with her thumbs and the drone levitated before us. She made it fly over the heads of the congregation and showed me on the screen in her handset a bird's eye view of all the Brylcreemed combovers and Christmas perms.

'Do you want a go?' Sarah said.

'Me?' I stuttered.

Sarah didn't wait for an answer. She shoved the controller into my hand and babbled a load of technical jargon at me – like, this is up and down, this is left and right – before leaving me, a self-confessed techno-tit, in charge of an expensive bit of surveillance kit.

'Oh my gosh,' I said as I watched the drone career around the church, swooping down on the congregation like a seagull trying to steal chips at the seaside. 'Sarah, this is wonderful, but I think you better—'

Just then on the screen I caught a glimpse of Alfie who was, it seemed, a little too eager to follow my instruction to keep practising, and was currently whizzing down the aisle towards Sarah and I. 'Careful!' I said jovially, still trying to be the MC the audience expected me to be. But it was too late. Alfie slammed into me, I lost what little control I had of the drone and it dive-bombed into the organ pipes, which resounded with an appropriately doleful boom.

There was a moment of stunned silence, until Erin cried out, 'My ring!'

She wasn't sore after all that sex she was getting these days, she was referring to and racing towards the advent ring, a wreath of dried flowers in which stand four candles, one more of which is lit with every Sunday that passes in advent. This means that the first candle to be lit gets rather small by Christmas Day, unless you put four new ones in the wreath every week. Liz, my therapod steward at St John's preferred her candles like her cranberry juice, fresh every week. Erin, however, here at St Augustine's liked the unevenness that would result from each candle burning longer than the next. It showed the passing of time better, she thought, which added to her seasonal excitement. With Liz's track record with wine and bread, I was less open to any ideas she had, but in the case of an advent ring I should have embraced her methods throughout my churches.

The first candle of Erin's ring had burned so low it had ignited the wreath in which it stood. But, like a boss, Erin grabbed the flaming crown, ran across to the fire exit and tossed the whole thing out into the car park.

The car park?

Where cars full of petrol are?

'Erin!' I said, racing outside and scooping up the burning bush, which unfortunately gave me no divine instruction, so I ran back inside with it, drowning it in the font, an action which I often felt like doing to screaming babies as they grabbed my lapel mic, pulled my hair and vomited on me during baptisms.

For a moment there I was a hero, saving the church from being razed to the ground, which was handy in deflecting attention from Sarah, who was mourning the damage to her ridiculously lavish gift. But I'm sure her parents, being the Christians they purported to be, would use this as a moment to reflect, at this time of all times, on what Jesus said in Luke, Chapter 12:

'Life does not consist in the abundance of possessions.'

THIRTY-SIX

The Church Anniversary Lunch last year was unforgettable, but not for the delicious roasted veg couscous I brought.

'I don't trust that foreign muck,' Reg was heard to mutter as he eyed my contribution before chowing down on the pork pies his wife had brought.

It was my first such lunch at St Augustine's. I was doing my duty, working my way round the church hall, circulating like white blood cells around the body of our congregation, trying to make everyone feel good, included and welcome, making small talk about the service that had just happened, gritting my teeth as everyone talked about the hymns and not the sermon, when I saw Ray sitting by himself. I went over to sit with him, which was no chore as I have a soft spot for him. Ray was such an unassuming chap, but he had a twinkle in his eye too. He was in his early forties and loved heavy rock music, travelling the length and breadth of the country to see his favourite bands. He was a real connoisseur of the genre and could regale you with all manner of fascinating facts about it when given the chance. But the thing I loved most about Ray was his mum, Angie. Ray came with his mum to church most Sundays. But when I first met Angie she was alone and struggling with her iPad. My techno-tittery barred me from using drones, but wasn't so bad that I couldn't get behind the wheel of a tablet. I downloaded *The Bible in a Year* podcast for her and every Sunday thereafter she would find me at church and tell me what she'd heard that week. After a year of listening, she'd decided that God was a dick. 'He's a schizophrenic, genocidal, sexist tyrant,' she said. 'But Jesus. He's alright.'

I saw how Angie wrestled with her faith. For her it was real, it was her life, and to me she was a true Christian. If I had been single I would have married Ray just to have Angie as a mother-in-law.

At the lunch, Angie was absent, sick I think, but this provided Ray with an opportunity he needed. I began to ask the usual questions, how are you, etc, but before I could even finish my sentence, he told me he had a problem he needed to talk to me about. Serious pastoral head was suddenly switched on as I could see from the intensity in his eyes that this was important and not about the appearance of 'While Shepherds Watched Their Flock By Night' in today's paeanic playlist.

'It's about Trudy.'

I hoped she wasn't sick too.

'Well, I suppose, it's about both of us really. But...' Ray looked up to make sure we weren't in earshot of anyone else and mumbled, 'She's pregnant and...' he quickly added before I waded in with some congratulatory platitude, '...we can't keep... it... She needs to have an abortion. Her medical history means if she has a baby she won't survive.'

'OK,' I said gently.

'But I wasn't sure how you felt about abortions, you know, as a priest. Please don't judge me.'

That stung; the idea that I might not have given Ray the impression that I wouldn't judge him. I touched his shoulder and said, 'Ray, I'm not here to judge you. I'm here to love you and help you through this difficult time and I'm honoured you've shared this with me.'

At those words I felt his shoulder relax and in that moment I knew how alone he and Trudy must have been feeling.

'Why don't you go and be with Trudy?' I said. 'Go home. You don't need to be here. I'll come over as soon as I can this afternoon and we'll work out what to do together, OK?'

He nodded and slipped out before anyone could ask him why he was leaving so soon.

*

No wonder they didn't know where to turn. It only took a few phone calls to find out there were no resources to help women in Trudy's predicament in this backwater town. Ray and Trudy sat on the stairs of their maisonette like two naughty children as I sat at their telephone table dialling clinics. I had no idea what I was doing – just like Ray and Trudy – but they were in such distress that they just needed someone to take the reins for a minute, to hold their hand and fumble forward through the dark with them.

Even if there had been an NHS clinic nearby willing to help, Trudy would have wrestled with the idea of attending. The grapevine was faster than fibre broadband in these parts and there were people – family, mainly – who just couldn't find out what she was doing. Her life, Ray reliably informed me, wouldn't be worth living if they did. Angie was so desperate for a grandchild she would have been livid if she ever found out Trudy had an abortion. Trudy already wasn't good enough for her boy – is any woman ever good enough for mummy's little soldier? – and this would be the final nail in the coffin of their rocky relationship.

After two hours of talking to professionals from clinics far and wide I was beginning to understand the process involved in a termination: two appointments, two days and £600 as the NHS can't fund all the abortions required in this country.

A week later I was wrestling with my Sat Nav, Trudy sitting quietly beside me in the passenger seat, as I tried to find a car park close to the clinic in the middle of a city I had never been to before, four hours from Trudy's home. We found ourselves walking through what seemed to us a maze of streets and then, just round the corner from a church with a billboard outside that announced how it was *Serving the city*, in something of a daze we found our final destination. I wondered if there were other young women like Trudy who attended that church and then popped around here to the abortion clinic, which served the city in its own way.

It was on a run-down street that would be more fitting a home for a dodgy tanning salon or massage parlour where tanning and massaging were the last things that went on. Trudy had been told to give only her initials through the buzzer at the door, which then opened with a guillotine clang. The first thing we saw on entering the clinic was an unmissable sign saying *No children allowed*. The irony of it slapped me in the face. It was like a sick joke, but, of course, this was no place for children; little humans bouncing around were the last thing the women sat here needed to see.

Trudy was given a yellow card with a number 21 on it and told that she would be referred to by that colour and number for the rest of the day. Like giving her initials at the buzzer it was all about confidentiality, of course, but it was awfully impersonal too. We sat together and she took out her phone and did what most of us do in an awkward situation, lose ourselves in anti-social social media to take our minds off waiting, to keep the fear of the unknown at bay. She didn't want to look around and be faced with this miserable reality of hers. I, however, couldn't resist gazing around the oppressively small room; at the water cooler with a notice over it: *Please drink enough water so you have a full bladder for the scan*; at the posters around the wall offering counselling and advice on safe sex; at the numbers to call if you're in an abusive relationship. But what struck me most was the vast array of women who were there:

The girl so young and carefree, she danced into the waiting room taking it all in her ripped denim stride. She had the smudge of a smile on her face and it was clear that this wasn't her first time here. She casually held her yellow 25 card like a cigarette, crossed her legs, tossed back her long blonde hair and took out her phone.

The middle-aged woman quietly sobbing in the corner, not the usual demographic of customer here, I thought, until Red 13 came out of a consultation room and sat next to her, saying in an audible whisper, 'Mum, I've left it too late. They can't do it. I'm stuck with it.' A conversation ensued which I tried desperately not to hear. It's not my business, I told myself. But in this tiny space, it was an effort not to eavesdrop.

The three young Muslim women and their chaperones, the girls looking frightened and lost and the chaperones looking matriarchal and caring.

The Romanian woman, who when called, made it clear that she needed her interpreter to go in with her. The clinic staff said apologetically to the interpreter that she couldn't join her client. The interpreter interpreted and the Romanian turned a whiter shade of pale as tears started to roll down her porcelain cheeks. The nurse took her hand and gave it a comforting squeeze and the interpreter said something in Romanian to her, which was most probably words of encouragement: 'It will be OK.' It's amazing how our bodies do most of the talking so that we can understand each other without speaking the same language.

I took in all these disparate faces and wondered where God was. I looked again from Ripped Jeans Girl to Crying Mother to her daughter to the Romanian to the three Muslim women and then to Trudy, and I realised that God was here in this place and probably more so than in the church around the corner. I was desperate to talk to all of these women and tell them, 'Though you walk through this valley of the shadow of death...' and this was literally a valley of the shadow of death '...God is here with you and you need not be afraid.'

'Yellow 21.'

The words jolted me from my thoughts. That was Trudy's number.

I whispered, 'I'll be out here waiting for you.'

She managed to smile at me briefly before following the nurse inside.

Incognito without my dog-collar, I prayed quietly, as I sat, for all the staff working here and all the women coming in and out, and then I too got my phone out and started playing a mind-numbing game.

After what felt like an age, Trudy came out and sat next to me with her eyes pooling and whispered, 'I need to put this inside me, but I can't do it.' She uncurled her hand revealing a glove, a small paper pot with a pill in it and another paper pot with some KY Jelly.

'Can't the nurses help you?' I frowned looking around.

Apparently they were too busy trying to get through the backlog of patients. Her allotted time had come to an end.

'They just said do it on my way out.' Trudy looked lost.

'Come on, I'll help you. I didn't get my first aid badge at Guides for nothing,' I winked.

I strode into the toilet off the waiting room but was arrested by the state of it. It was filthy with discarded gloves and paper pots littering a floor smeared with unholy substances. But the last thing that Trudy needed was for me to freak out so I smiled at her and said, 'You're getting your collection money's worth out of me today.'

Trudy laughed, loudly and briefly.

As I helped Trudy get the pill up inside her, crouched among the debris, the dirt and the dinginess of this toilet, it came to me that this was probably how Mary felt when she was giving birth in similarly insalubrious circumstances. The debris, the dirt and dinginess of a stable, or barn or wherever she was. And that brought crashing home to me the power of the Incarnation, the moment when God took human form in the birth of Jesus. God is here, even here, I thought, because this is where God is needed most. In the debris, the dirt and the dinginess of an abortion clinic toilet. God is here.

*

We came back the next day, knowing that this was going to be the harder of the two days but feeling oddly buoyant because we knew where to go and how the system worked. We were old hands at this now. Trudy gave her initials through the intercom like a pro and, once inside, picked a new card. 'Today, Matthew, I'm going to be... Red 11.' The wait wasn't too long this time. Red 11 was soon called in and fifteen minutes later Trudy returned, desperate to leave. We picked up our stuff and went to reception for the most bizarre action I had ever witnessed in my life. Trudy took out her purse and handed over the £600 in cash her and Ray had scraped together. The staff behind the desk counted it out and asked if she wanted a receipt. It seemed to me a strange concept to give a receipt for a termination. It was as if it was merely a transaction. For the staff who worked here every day, of course, it was. But for those who hand over the money, why would they want a paper tombstone, a souvenir of the trauma they were about to inflict on their body?

As we left, I handed the staff at reception a card. They looked at me with surprise so I explained, 'It's just a thank you card for everything you do, your kindness and your help.'

The receptionist took it from me and a look of weary appreciation came over her. I suppose they didn't get thanked too often. It wasn't *the done thing*. But fuck that! I was determined to spread a little of God's love about this valley of the shadow of death.

*

The nurses had given Trudy a sanitary towel but I'd brought a back-up towel and one of my granddad's surplus incontinence nappies. I'd never done this before and had no idea what was about to happen but I'd read a few things so thought I'd prepare for the worst. We drove through the city, me trying to make small talk, Trudy nodding politely until we found the motorway that would take us home.

That was when Trudy started shivering. It was a cold December day, though inside the car I thought it was warm enough. However, Trudy couldn't stop shaking, so I put the heating on full blast, yet still she couldn't get warm. I baked in the car for a good hour (actually it was a pretty bad hour) then pulled into a McDonald's to get us something to eat. We hadn't eaten all day.

'Can you manage something?' I asked.

She nodded. 'I have to try.'

'Good, coz I'm bloody starving.' I must have been to go into a McDonald's, but I had a desolate three hour stretch of the M1 before me – what else could we do?

McWhatevers in hand, Trudy clearly didn't want or need to talk about what had happened today, so we chatted about anything else and soon landed on the topic of Ray.

'How did you meet?' I asked.

Trudy smiled, her eyes glazed over and she said, 'It was Mother's Day. I had taken my mum out to a restaurant for dinner and we were seated next to this bloke who was clearly taking his mum out for a Mother's Day treat too, like most people in the restaurant. That was Ray and Angie.'

'No way,' I said, enchanted already.

'Well, you know what it's like,' Trudy went on. 'They pack you in way too tightly so you can't help but overhear everyone else's conversation. Ray was telling his mum about this Iron Maiden gig he really wanted to go to in a couple of weeks, but he was gutted because his friend couldn't make it and now he had a spare ticket and no one to go with. He was wondering if he'd even go. I couldn't believe it when I heard this. My favourite band is Iron Maiden too, you see. So I leant over – I couldn't resist – and told him. Told him I know I'm a complete stranger, but if it means we both get to see them, then I'd happily buy his spare ticket and go with him. He agreed and then...'

'The rest is history,' I said. 'How romantic. I love it.'

Just then Trudy paled.

'I'll be right back,' she growled.

She dashed to the toilet and left me looking about the service station at all the people who seemed to be going about their lives without a care in the world and I thought of dear old Eric, once stuck on the mountaintop of his grief.

Before long Trudy came back to the table. She was unsteady on her feet.

'Could you get some paper bags from the counter, please? I need to go to the car.'

I gave her the keys and asked a baffled staff member for some empty paper bags. I grabbed a bottle of water too and gave it to Trudy when I caught her up.

'You OK?'

She frowned. 'I just honked my guts up,' she said. 'It's as if my body knows it needs to get rid of something and isn't sure what, so it just settled on the obvious thing first, the Macky-D's.'

We shared an illicit giggle and I handed her the bags, the function of which was now perfectly clear.

'Nothing else has happened. Yet,' Trudy said apprehensively as we got in the car.

We listened to some music and Trudy watched the world go by as I drove more carefully than I'd ever driven in my life – Constable Five Cameras would be pleased. I felt like the donkey carrying Mary, knowing I had a precious cargo to deliver, the difference being, Mary was bringing the Christ child into a broken world, I was carrying a broken child to Christ.

Then suddenly Trudy gripped the car door and yelped, 'It's happening.'

'Shit, shit, OK. Are you OK?' I said, my eyes darting back and forth from the road to Trudy.

'No, I'm not OK,' she said, examining her crotch. 'This sanitary towel is not going to cut it.'

I grabbed the towel from the back seat whilst negotiating the road and handed it to Trudy. She immediately pulled down her trousers and made a makeshift pad out of it.

Up ahead I saw another set of golden arches glowing in the sky like the star of Bethlehem. I thanked God for McDonald's – not something I think I'd ever done before, or since, and pulled into the car park.

Trudy was distressed as her body tried to turn itself inside out. I switched off the engine and pulled my granddad's nappy from the back seat.

'I know it's not ideal, but I have this. We can put it over your knickers and under your jeans and we'll get you inside and sort you out.'

We shimmied the nappy over her pants and put her jeans on without fastening them up. I gave her my coat to hide the unzipped trousers and gave her my arm to steady her as we walked inside. I delivered her to the toilets and went to get a wad of napkins and a drink from the counter. When I got back, the cubicle was locked.

'Do you need any help?' I cooed, peering under the door from where a soft sob came.

I saw a pool of blood around Trudy's feet and then a gushing sound made me straighten up. It was a sound I'd never heard before. It wasn't the sound of piss or diarrhoea. This was the sound of the lining of a woman's womb being flushed out of her vagina. I crouched down and passed a wad of napkins under the door. Trudy used them to start mopping up the puddle of blood around her.

Some deep breaths later, she was out of the toilet and I helped her back to the car, so many napkins in hand the counter staff must have thought I was a really messy eater.

'Those sanitary towels are like a fart in the wind,' she gasped. 'There's so much blood. They aren't going to do anything.'

'Tampons?' I offered lamely.

'The nurses said not to use tampons, but they wouldn't do anything anyway. I don't know what to do.'

'We're over halfway now,' I reassured her. 'There's a Sainsbury's not far from here if I remember rightly. Let's go there and stock up on everything we need to get you through this.'

Perhaps I hadn't remembered rightly. Or perhaps it was how tense I was on Trudy's behalf. Either way, the drive to Sainsbury's seemed to take forever. Every now and again, Trudy would lift herself up out of the seat and brace herself for what I could only imagine was another shedding of her uterus wall.

I thought of the menstruating woman in the Bible, who'd been bleeding for twelve years. *Twelve years?* I'm pissed off for a few days every month when the cramps and the indignity of it all happens. Non-stop for over a decade and Spencer might end up with a knife through his chest – from me or himself. No doctor could heal the woman, she had spent everything she had on trying to find a solution, not just for her physical comfort, but no doubt because of the social stigma, as scribes and Pharisees bashed her with passages from the Torah which stated how unclean menstrual blood is. So when she found herself in a crowd close to Jesus she plucked up the courage to touch the hem of his cloak because she believed it would heal her. She was right. She was healed, rewarded for her faith.

That geyser-like sound from the McToilet echoed in my mind and it crystalised for me how menstrual blood is not something to be reviled, but the source of all life. The Incarnation – God made real, through the messiness of our lives, through the bloodiness of our traumas – the Incarnation was in the world and the world was made through this very same being, then in the form of a baby in a manger, a baby created, as we all are, via the medium of menstrual blood. The Incarnation came to those who claimed to represent Him and worship Him, but they did not recognise or receive Him. If Jesus came into the world right now in the twenty-first century he would not be hanging out with the 'great and the good'. He would be in the red-light districts, the skid rows, he would be hanging with the drug dealers and the paedophiles, the bankers screwing the economy, the politicians screwing the people. He would be where he was needed. And those who notice, who see the Incarnation in the most unlikely of places and accept Him into their lives, they are the children of God. Here Trudy was, horrifically shedding her womb and the foetus that had been growing inside her in the passenger seat of my car, yet all I could feel was the overwhelming love and presence of God for her, for the baby and for me.

*

We pulled into the Sainsbury's car park and I almost had to carry Trudy into the disabled toilet. Once she was safely in there, I ran around the shop grabbing the most absorbent things I could find in the feminine section, then, back in the toilet, I knocked on the door.

'Only me,' I said in hushed tones before gently pushing open the door.

Trudy was sitting on the toilet with her head in her hands, her jeans, my granddad's incontinence pad, her knickers and the pathetic sanitary towel the clinic had given her nestled around her feet.

I knelt down, opened the bag of stuff I'd bought and said, 'You'll be surprised how being clean for a moment will make you feel better,' as I handed her some wipes.

She got to work on herself, I got to work cleaning the floor and, while I was down there, I placed a wad of tissues in Trudy's knickers to soak up some of the blood. I was struck by how thick the blood was. It had formed a seal with the fabric and allowed a pool to form in the gusset. There was something beguiling about it.

As I helped Trudy change and clean up, I felt overwhelmed with a sense of privilege that I, a trusted stranger, could be here for her in this moment of need. She no longer had her parents, no family, and Ray couldn't get the time off work. There are benefits to not working a 9-5; being able to drop things relatively easily for pastoral problems. As that sense of privilege washed over me, the Christmas story made more sense than ever before.

If Mary had given birth in the 21st Century, it would have been in a service station because there was no room in the Premier Inn. She would be in a disabled toilet just like this one crumpled in an exhausted heap, and those who came to pay homage would not be hallucinating shepherds or royal astronomers, but the immigrant cleaners, who barely spoke a word of English but in a previous life in a war-torn country worked in medicine or law. The Word made flesh would have been wrapped in paper towels and laid in a sink. It had to be that way so that when people like Trudy find themselves walking through the dark in the valley of the shadow of death, they can see the Light, the Light that shines for all people; people like Trudy, because the Incarnation was born into the chaos, sorrow and pain that she was inhabiting right now.

*

Somehow, we made it home. Ray was waiting anxiously at the door as we arrived. He was eager to take over caring duties from me, so I left them to it for the night.

When I got back to my manse, I was greeted by the cat, threw my bags on the floor and walked straight into the bathroom to have the longest shower of my life. As the warm water massaged my body, I noticed a trickle of blood flow down my leg. It was as if my body was responding in empathy with Trudy's; my own period had started a few days early. The blood mingled with the water by my feet and I thought of Jesus on the cross; *blood and water* flowing from his body when a soldier pierced his side with a spear [John, 19:34]. I thought of the 15th Century atonement theory: the blood of Christ washes us free from our sin; sin that was so awful, so heavy, that there was nothing we humans could do ourselves, no sacrifice we could make to quench the wrath God felt about it. The only thing that would make amends in God's opinion, according to this theory, was the sacrifice of his only son.

What a load of bollocks!

I cannot underline enough how fucked up that theory is. If that was any other parent's attitude to their son, we'd all be calling social services. Talk about a safeguarding issue! Call Childline now! To me, there is a far more realistic interpretation of the events of the crucifixion and one that is not so dangerous, one which doesn't feed the minds of extremists who think blowing up innocent people these days is some kind of divine sacrifice. When good people, true altruists, pure forgiving souls, walk the earth like Jesus did they tend to be persecuted by the religious or political powers that be, whose greedy hold on society is threatened by their very existence; or they are shunned by ordinary people who fear such alien traits in the broken world they/we live in. My job as a priest is to try to fan the flames of goodness that still reside somewhere in the moral dubiousness of us all, to encourage us to be the change we want to see, to get *back to the garden*, as Joni Mitchell said. And I don't think that had

194

ever made more sense to me than it did after that surreal day with Trudy as I stood leaning against the shower wall with the blood and the water flowing from me. Never had Jesus's awful ending seemed so tangible to me, never had it made so much sense. The sense being, that it was senseless.

*

I stayed in touch with Ray and Trudy over the following months, particularly with Ray, who I'd see at church. I can't say I'm very good at remembering dates, I'm not even sure when I got married, but December 19th was etched onto my brain forever.

After church one Sunday the following November, I pulled Ray quietly to one side and said, 'Christmas is coming and so is the 19th. It's not going to be easy for you. Would you like me to do you a little service to mark the birth and the time that has gone by?'

Ray's jaw tightened. He thought for a moment. 'Um… Can I think about it?'

'Of course you can,' I said.

'Only, you know, Trudy's not really religious.'

'I can do a non-religious one with perhaps a sprinkling of God for you,' I smiled.

The next day Ray called me and said he and Trudy would like to accept my offer.

*

Not surprisingly, there isn't a liturgy in the Worship Book for those who've had an abortion, so I trawled through the internet to see what I could find. I found a huge gap in the market. There was a myriad of prayers available for the 'damned and condemned souls' of those who have terminated a pregnancy, but for those seeking forgiveness, comfort and peace, there was not much out there. After much prayer and silence, I came up with a simple liturgy for someone who was seeking solace. Writing the religious service gave me a grounding, and only after that could I set to work on writing a non-religious one.

When that was done, I called up Erin.

195

'I need to book the church on the 19th for a private service,' I said vaguely.

'Great. Let me just check I'm free to steward,' she chirped.

'No, no, Erin, it's fine. It's a very small thing and the family don't want any fuss.'

'Ah,' she said. 'I'll just hang around the back then in case you need me.'

I swallowed my irritation then smiled down the phone. 'No, no, really, it's fine. It's a very private thing. The family don't want anyone else but me to be there.'

I loved Erin, but she was as discreet as a reality TV star desperate for likes. Trudy did not need word of this service getting out into the community. The silence on the end of the line now resounded with Erin's disappointment. So I threw her a bone, though a wrench would have been more useful.

'But I do need you to put the heating on an hour or so before the service. Make it nice and warm in there for us, would you?' No one ever tells you about such mundane things at theological college. A few teeth-chattering services had taught me this particular lesson.

*

On the 19th I went down to the church early. I felt like a verger preparing for a coronation. I wanted everything to be perfect. Erin was still there when I came in.

'Are you sure you don't need me to…?' she gestured limply at the back of the church.

'No, no. It's better if you go now, you know,' I said, trying not to sound too mysterious, otherwise Erin would have circled the church like a fly round a picnic.

I found a small table and put it directly in front of the altar. I put a nice cloth over it, added some candles (with nothing flammable nearby this time), a small cross and a little olive-wood carving of a shepherd holding a lamb that I had at home. I moved some of the Christmas decorations which were already in the church onto the table: pine cones, tartan bows, little bells and holly branches. I placed three chairs in front of the table and dimmed the lights.

At the appointed time, Ray and Trudy shuffled in like haggard old people, but as they took in the table adorned just for them, they unfurled themselves, touched by the effort I'd made in transforming the place. We chatted idly for a moment about nothing, then I suggested we sit and have a period of stillness before we began.

Silence filled the chapel and I felt the Holy Spirit dwell among us. Then I guided them through the service, acknowledging the past, the present and the future, with an opportunity to light candles and remember Freddie; I learnt that night of his name.

We listened to a piece of music I had chosen. It was called 'Vice Verses' by a rock band called Switchfoot, which I thought they would both appreciate. This song was stripped down to just acoustic guitar and a solitary vocal, and was all the more powerful for it. As the Californian voice reverberated nostalgically from the stone arches above us, I watched Trudy huddle close to Ray and I found myself worrying that the heating wasn't high enough. Then a line or two from the song penetrated my thoughts.

You've got your babies, I've got my hearses,
Every blessing comes with a set of curses.

'How true, how true,' I said to myself, and as Ray put his arm around Trudy, I was so glad they had each other in this world of blessings and curses.

We priests tend to lament the commercialisation of Christmas, the rush, hype and hysteria of it all, and as I sat listening to this piece of music, the story of the birth of Christ was revealed more sharply than ever. The birth of a Saviour would result in catastrophic death. But the memory of the dead for so many is forgotten and hidden away by so called Christmas cheer – no one wants Auntie Edna crying in a corner because on the 24th December 1956 her baby was killed in a car crash. Yet among the tinsel and baubles, the glitter and gluttony, the reality of life and death was here before me; the tragedy of masked pain and heartache in a land of pretend joy and cheer.

What was I doing? More than any other time of year, my diary was packed; stuffed with services where I would be expected to be an entertainer, a master of ceremonies, because it's Christmas and that's what the punters want. The gospel narrative of the birth of Christ, however, tells a different story; one of dirt, dinge and destruction; of grief and gnawing pain. In the stillness of the chapel right then I realised, this was the most important service I would do during this Advent, because it was the most real.

*

At the end of the service, I showed Ray and Trudy out, then sat back down in front of the flickering candles and wept. I cried for everything that had happened to them. For women who are forgotten and struggling at Christmas. For those who feel they cannot talk about abortions because no one likes to hear about such 'unpalatable' things. For the staff who work in the clinics. For families who support women through these times. And most of all, for those who feel judged by the church. I cried out a prayer in between my sobs; praying that I would be given the courage to minister to those who needed God and, above all, those who needed God and didn't know it.

THIRTY-SEVEN

The church at its best is a family. Like all families we have the mad old uncle ranting his bigoted nonsense in the corner, we have disagreements and we fall out, but essentially we are all there because we are looking to belong. We are the odd-shaped pegs that don't fit into the neat square holes of conventional society. We are the misfits and the outsiders, the marginalised and the vulnerable. And when you examine yourself for more than a minute, you'll find that you too are in some way on the outside. It was the misfits and the outsiders that Jesus gravitated to and stood up for, as we all should. Yes, the Bible is in many ways a fantastical crock of shite at worst, allegorical at best. If you struggle with the idea of God being a supernatural being or even a white bearded man, then think of God as a way of referring to that ember of goodness that still resides somewhere in the moral dubiousness of us all; and the kingdom of God, not as some realm above the stars, but the Edenic state we could attain on Earth if we grasped and practised the teaching of the Messiah. Jesus, the real-life person, was clearly a beautiful human being with a simple message: love your neighbour and don't be a dick. Why would anyone not want to get on board that train?

***

Acknowledgements

Laura would like to thank…

Spencer, for allowing me to tell our batshit story.
Katy, my sister without whom I am incomplete.
All my college friends for getting me through the craziness
of that shithole.
My Churches – thank you for accepting me as me, and for all
the fun we have together.
Warren, for believing in me and my story, and crafting the
words to bring it to life.
Armley Press, for taking a risk with me.
Jesus – you still put up with me despite it all, you're the best.
x

Warren would like to thank…

Laura, for trusting me, a white working-class male atheist,
with your story. We are *poles* apart, demographically
speaking, but I admire the way you saw how that was the
point. Indeed, that is the point of storytelling – empathy.
Thanks for the empathy you show to your flock and thanks
for allowing me to exercise mine.
John and Mick at Armley Press, for walking where other
publishers fear to tread.
Friends and family, for the eternal cheerleading.
And to VW… for your assistance. Ha!

Armley Press would like to thank…

Irene Bendler.
June from Leeds Pole Dance Studio, Bramley.

Other recent titles from Armley Press

Soldiers
Frederick Turner
'Well recommended'

Before the Gulf
John Lake
'A great read on so many levels'

The Heat of the Summer
Liam Randles
'A truly engrossing novel'

Dying is the Last Thing You Ever Want to Do
Michael Yates
'Gripping, intelligent, authentic... and tremendous fun!'

Whoosh!
Ray Brown
'I laughed out loud... then laughed out loud again'

The Last Sane Man on Earth
Nathan O'Hagan
'A satirical, poignant and hilarious modern classic'

Sex & Death and other stories
Ivor Tymchak
'Surprising, disturbing and funny'

Thurso
P. James Callaghan
'Unflinching and raw... a "make you think" dark debut'

www.armleypress.com

Milton Keynes UK
Ingram Content Group UK Ltd.
UKHW051150240324
439902UK00004B/156